The Philosophy of Rabindranath Tagore

Bloomsbury Introductions to World Philosophies

Bloomsbury Introductions to World Philosophies delivers primers reflecting exciting new developments in the trajectory of world philosophies. Instead of privileging a single philosophical approach as the basis of comparison, the series provides a platform for diverse philosophical perspectives to accommodate the different dimensions of cross-cultural philosophizing. While introducing thinkers, texts and themes emanating from different world philosophies, each book, in an imaginative and path-breaking way, makes clear how it departs from a conventional treatment of the subject matter.

Titles in the Series:

A Practical Guide to World Philosophies, by Monika Kirloskar-Steinbach and Leah Kalmanson

Daya Krishna and Twentieth-Century Indian Philosophy, by Daniel Raveh

Māori Philosophy, by Georgina Tuari Stewart

Philosophy of Science and The Kyoto School, by Dean Anthony Brink

Tanabe Hajime and the Kyoto School, by Takeshi Morisato

African Philosophy, by Pascah Mungwini

The Zen Buddhist Philosophy of D. T. Suzuki, by Rossa Ó Muireartaigh

Sikh Philosophy, by Arvind-Pal Singh Mandair

The Philosophy of the Brahma-sūtra, by Aleksandar Uskokov
The Philosophy of the Yogasūtra, by Karen O'Brien-Kop
The Life and Thought of H. Odera Oruka, by Gail M. Presbey
Mexican Philosophy for the 21st Century, by Carlos Alberto Sánchez
Buddhist Ethics and the Bodhisattva Path, by Stephen Harris
Contextualizing Angela Davis, by Joy James

The Philosophy of Rabindranath Tagore

Thinking Across Cultures

Ramin Jahanbegloo

BLOOMSBURY
NEW DELHI • LONDON • OXFORD • NEW YORK • SYDNEY

BLOOMSBURY INDIA
Bloomsbury Publishing India Pvt. Ltd
Second Floor, LSC Building No. 4, DDA Complex, Pocket C–6&7,
Vasant Kunj, New Delhi 110070

BLOOMSBURY, BLOOMSBURY ACADEMIC INDIA and the Diana logo are
trademarks of Bloomsbury Publishing Plc

First published in India 2025
First published in Great Britain 2025

Series design by Louise Dugdale
Cover image © Abi Afandi / Adobe Stock

This edition published with permission from Bloomsbury Publishing Plc,
50 Bedford Square, London, WC1B3DP, UK

A catalogue record for this book is available from the British Library.
A catalog record for this book is available from the Library of Congress.

ISBN: 978-93-61311-75-8

Series:
Bloomsbury Introductions to World Philosophies

Typeset by Newgen KnowledgeWorks Pvt. Ltd., Chennai, India
Printed and bound in India by Replika Press Pvt. Ltd.

In memory of Sudhir Kakar

Contents

Series Editor Preface

The introductions we include in the World Philosophies series take a single thinker, theme or text and provide a close reading of them. What defines the series is that these are likely to be people or traditions that you have not yet encountered in your study of philosophy. By choosing to include them, you broaden your understanding of ideas about the self, knowledge and the world around us. Each book presents unexplored pathways into the study of world philosophies. Instead of privileging a single philosophical approach as the basis of comparison, each book accommodates the many different dimensions of cross-cultural philosophizing. While the choice of terms used by the individual volumes may indeed carry a local inflection, they encourage critical thinking about philosophical plurality. Each book strikes a balance between locality and globality.

The Philosophy of Rabindranath Tagore is a fresh attempt to interpret the intricate connection between spiritual beauty, metaphysical truth and humanism in the thinking of Rabindranath Tagore. Ramin Jahanbegloo elucidates how Tagore weaves together spirituality, aesthetics and a love of humanity to understand culture as an everchanging, contingent way of making sense of being human. Positing Tagore as our contemporary, Jahanbegloo invites the reader to engage in a Tagorean intercultural dialogue so that philosophy as the practice of decency can be made possible. Deeply committed to regenerating their cultures, dialogue participants are per this understanding ready to engage in creative, critical, anti-systematic thinking in order to regenerate their living cultures.

Foreword

S. Irfan Habib

The best way to describe Rabindranath Tagore and his philosophy is to see him through a cosmopolitan perspective, where narrowness and prejudice of mind did not exist. During the past few decades, he had been viewed primarily as a Bengali intellectual, poet and cultural figure, while his philosophy of life remained beyond such restraints. Despite the fact that he set new standards in Bangla literature through his poetry and prose, his philosophical vision remained internationalist. He was never constrained by the territorial or nationalist boundaries, a remarkable feat during the anti-colonial struggle. This little book by Ramin Jahanbegloo, an Iranian philosopher based in India, fits perfectly well within the internationalist vision of Tagore. It rather goes on to reiterate the celebration of Tagore's cosmopolitan world view who never saw himself restricted by any sectarian or national identity. He was himself conscious of the fact that the people of Bengal 'are neglectful towards people of other regions', and thus they need to overcome narrow provincialism.[1] In his scathing comment on the prevailing narrow provincialism in Bengal Tagore wrote:

> The chief weakness of the people of Bengal is self-pride, which is why they are unhappy if they do not hear all the time words of praise … This vanity, hunger for flattery, obscures their vision and they do not perceive others clearly. We deprive ourselves on account of this blindness.[2]

Tagore received huge criticism for such harsh words, which he spoke at the Bengali literary conference in Banaras in 1923. However, his humanism broke all barriers during his lifetime and continues to do so even now despite immense cultural, intellectual and political strains.

We normally say this about many people that he was ahead of his time, given the nature of the profile, but for Tagore it is not merely a cliché. In his case, it is truly a fact that he had the courage and vision to say things which were almost impossible to utter in public. He was much misunderstood and maligned, particularly when he strongly spoke about cosmopolitanism in the times of anti-colonial struggle. Tagore was not one who merely wrote about the cosmopolitan idea; he actually was one of those privileged people who could afford to live a cosmopolitan life. Between 1878 and 1932, Tagore travelled to more than thirty countries and many of them more than once. And he did not travel only to Europe and America but also to many Asian countries. In 1927, he travelled with some friends for four months to Java, Bali, Kuala Lumpur, Malacca, Penang, Siam and Singapore. This resulted in a travelogue called *Jatri* in 1929. In April 1932, Tagore, intrigued by the Persian mystic Hafez, was hosted by Reza Shah Pahlavi.[3] His travel meetings with many outstanding scientists, poets, writers, philosophers and several other artists are well known. For a mind like Tagore, this exposure made a seminal impact on his philosophy and politics.

In the words of Michael Collins, 'Living during the high period of anti-colonial nationalism in India – and yet espousing the ideal of "universal man" – Tagore was inevitably portrayed by some of his more nationalist-minded contemporaries as insufficiently patriotic and unduly influenced by the west.'[4] He was not patriotic enough for some because he had some high-profile non-Indian friends, and he also questioned the traditional Hindu belief regarding overseas travel taboos. In those hyper-nationalist times, Tagore was one of the greatest internationalists around, who 'recognized the right of each nation to work out its own destiny, but he also proclaimed that national claims must never encroach upon our human obligations'.[5] We can see that the frivolous interpretations of nationalism or patriotism we come across today are not actually new; we sadly have a long history behind such farcical nationalist games. One of the most important messages to remember from Tagore is that 'love and respect for the ideals of one's own people is a positive virtue, while disrespect for the ideals and traditions of others is a crime against humanity'. He had the courage to proclaim that blind worship of the nation and the nation state contained the seeds of disaster for man.

We will see ahead in my foreword, as well as in the book by Ramin, in further detail that Tagore was much concerned about the life of the mind, which meant a life that spoke of isolation and privacy. Despite being a public figure from a young age, Tagore loved and longed for his solitude; he wrote about it several times. As Sabyasachi says, Tagore 'suffered from an intense feeling of loneliness right from his childhood'.[6] He expressed this feeling in his letter to his friend C. F. Andrews from New York in 1921: 'I am afraid I shall be rejected by my own people when I go back to India. My solitary cell is awaiting me in my motherland.'[7] His stress on the inner life of the mind will be seen in most of his vocations. It is particularly prominent in his engagements with education, where cultivation of mind took prominence and not mere 'carrying the loads of words on our folded backs'.

Several years before he founded Visva-Bharati, Tagore wrote in 1906 that

> freedom is essential to the mind in the period of growth, and it is richly provided by nature … Are children to be blamed for not having learnt problems of algebra and dates of history before coming into this world? And is that any reason for depriving them of air and light, of freedom and joy and turning their education into a punishment in every detail?[8]

Tagore's model of education located the young learners in the midst of nature and not get stuck inside the prison walls of a classroom. 'God intended children to be educated in the freedom of nature, and we defeat ourselves by defeating his intention.'[9]

This slim volume by Ramin engages with most concerns of Tagore like Man, God and Nature in his philosophy, his dialogue of cultures, his strong rebuttal of the nationalist creed, Tagore's educational ideas and also his agreements and disagreements with Gandhi. Tagore's diverse interests and vocations were deeply imbued with humanist values that have salience in all the chapters that Ramin takes up. Tagore was also concerned about the intellectual environment in India of his days, for which he held primarily the colonial education responsible. But more importantly, 'he pointed to the limitedness of the average Indian individual's life, i.e. life beyond the home'.[10] When we read or write about Tagore, we need to keep in mind the observations he made about the India of the 1920s. He said:

> It is difficult to achieve greatness of mind and character where our responsibility is diminutive and fragmentary, where our whole life occupies and affects an extremely limited area … We, in India, live in a narrow cage of petty interests, we do not believe that we have wings, for we have lost our sky; we chatter and hop and peck at one another, within the small range of our obstructed opportunities.[11]

Tagore was disenchanted with his countrymen for their lack of engagement with ideas, except in politics. Maybe this decade of the 1920s was politically too volatile, which led Tagore to make this observation. It saw the emergence of the first Gandhian mass movement and its sudden withdrawal due to Chauri Chaura violence, leading to a huge political disappointment and also communal violence. This radical change in the social, political and intellectual life of India and of many Indians led Tagore to make some serious observations. His disenchantment with communal divide is palpable in these lines where he says, 'A country where only religion can unite people is doomed. And the divisiveness such a country manufactures using religion is the most monstrous divisiveness of all.'[12]

Ramin very appropriately begins the introductory chapter by calling Tagore our contemporary. It is his intellectual richness and farsightedness that makes him our contemporary. His humanism pervades his entire corpus of prose, poetry, politics and art, which is obviously timeless. S. Radhakrishnan expressed a similar sentiment when he said that 'the popularity of the writings of Rabindranath Tagore shows that there is neither the east nor west in the realm of spirit, and that his work meets a general want and satisfies a universal demand'.[13] It is a remarkable feat that Tagore could keep his sanity intact despite living through some violent and tumultuous times, not only in India but also globally. He worked for

> the rebuilding of India, not on any narrow basis of creed, province, or language, but on the broad basis of India and her spiritual vision of universal love. Indians should work for the regeneration of India because they are all Indians ... The Hindu as well as the Muslim finds India to be the home of his noble ancestors; her earth contains the dust of his saints; she is his seat of righteousness and religion; in her progress lies his hope.[14]

Similar sentiment was expressed by Maulana Azad in his famous Congress presidential address in 1940 saying,

> eleven hundred years of common history have enriched India with our common creative and constructive achievements. Our languages, our poetry, our literature, our culture, our art, our dress, our manners and customs all bear the stamp of this common life.[15]

Azad was deeply influenced by Tagore's 'lofty humanism which arose above all sectarian and communal limitations ... the whole world became to him a home and he felt close affiliation with all humanity. This sense of kinship with the whole world is the essence of Indian culture and perhaps its greatest contribution to the world.'[16] While inaugurating the Visva-Bharati as a central university in 1951, Maulana reiterated that Tagore 'started this institution to provide a meeting place for the culture of the east and the west ... it was modern in spirit and welcomed the contributions which the west has made to the development of the human spirit. It was this combination of the past and the present which distinguished Santiniketan.'[17] This was, as a matter of fact, the essence of Tagore's philosophy of life and letters. He visualized the world as a shared space where only humanity matters and not race, religion, culture or language.

Rabindranath Tagore was born in 1861 in a family where organized religion hardly had any place. 'His family was located at the confluence of three cultures: the Hindu, the Islamic, and the British.'[18] His own faith, a faith that has been commented upon by several scholars from diverse philosophical vantage points, remained open and porous to engage with multiple influences. He was brought up in their family mansion at Jorasanko, a building that gives you goose bumps even now. It was built by his grandfather, 'Prince' Dwarkanath Tagore (1794–1846). The family was a world in itself, combining values of the past and the present in creative ways.[19] In one of the letters to his wife Rabindranath stated:

> We are totally different from other Bengalis in everything-in education and culture, in language, in temperament and habit.[20]

In matters of religion, his family was deeply under the spell of Rammohun Roy's monotheistic Brahmo Samaj, a nonconformist reform movement initiated by Roy against Hindu orthodoxy. Rabindranath acknowledged in his writings several times that Roy was his first inspiration, who, he wrote

> was the first great man of our age with comprehensiveness of mind to realize the fundamental unity in the Hindu, Muslim, and Christian cultures. He represented India in the fulness of truth based not upon rejection but on perfect comprehension. I follow him though he is practically rejected by my countrymen.[21]

Let us digress a bit and place ourselves in the contemporary times, almost one hundred years ahead of Tagore. He would have expressed similar anguish at the celebration of homogeneity and hatred for the 'other' being enthusiastically peddled today by many in Tagore's India. That fundamental unity or monotheism of Roy, which Tagore venerated, will almost turn him into an object of hate today. He rued that the countrymen rejected Roy in his times. Sadly, the same countrymen will reject Tagore today for his stress that the path of unity of mankind traversed by India over the centuries was the true Indian path to follow.

He was different from many Brahmos in his appreciation and interest in the medieval Indian religion, 'particularly the quotidian religious culture of the *nirguni sants* of north India that sometimes overtakes his attachment to early philosophical texts'.[22] These traits of Tagore make him significantly different from most other intellectuals of modern India. This also explains his attitude towards organized religions. Roy's Brahmo Samaj was indeed a dissent against them, but Tagore went a few steps ahead in explaining religion and its humanitarian foundations. He was probably the first one to present Kabir, the fifteenth-century radical poet and reformer, to the world in English translation, taking him beyond Indian borders. He was also 'instrumental in strengthening public interest in what he called the "*maramiyas*," mystic singers from rural Bengal as, for instance, the Bauls'.[23] As expected from Tagore, he stressed on Kabir's severe castigation 'of sectarianism, of Brahmanical dogmatism, irrational forms of worship, and radical inversion of conventionally accepted values or imageries'.[24]

Tagore, in one of his early articles, goes into his understanding of dharma, where he stresses that dharma requires that we consciously and willingly follow the eternal Truth that lies within Nature. He makes it abundantly clear that one of the primary duties (dharma) in this world is concern for others. Selfishness is quite contrary to the nature of our worldly duties.[25] For Tagore, religion, like natural light, was free and natural as well. It is the religion that is produced through some human contrivance that is something cluttered and complex. Ramin, while engaging with Tagore's idea of God, also writes that

> it is in Nature that Man has glimpses of God and the fulness of reality. Tagore's deep feeling for Nature is an expression of the unity of Man and God in the cosmic aspiration towards greater perfection. For Tagore, Man is in search of the everlasting joy and rhythm in the stream of Nature. Therefore, the invitation is there – always and eternal – from the world of Nature to the world of Man. (p. 23)

Tagore expressed his strong faith in nature quite early in 1895 when he wrote in a letter that

> my religion is natural religion and the method of worship I employ is worship of nature. Yesterday, I glanced upon a mother goat reclining with a lazy elegance on a grassy patch by the roadside. Seated next to it was the kid in a state of deep repose. On viewing this, there arose in me a feeling that was deep-seated, wondrous, and aesthetically fulfilling. I give this very feeling of mine the name of religion.[26]

He wrote in an article 'The Simple Ways of Religion' in 1903, explaining how natural religion has been disfigured. He says,

> Having been subjected to endless ritualism, meaningless acts, abstract conceptions and quaint imagination, it has become so obscure and unnatural that each day one man or another is able to create new and mutually conflicting sects out of this self-begotten fantasy. There now appears to be no end to the hostility, mutual bickering, and suspicion that such mutually conflicting claims have created.[27]

Tagore spoke essentially about Hinduism, but this is true about most religions across the world. He always prioritized human values and feelings above any ritualistic religious dogma. He wrote once in a letter, 'I do lose my patience when I find the god of the temple in competition with the God who resides in men. When touring Gaya, I noticed how a wealthy woman from Western India deposited a heap of precious coins at the feet of the local religious guide (panda): coins that came to be minted by snatching away food from hungry men.'[28] He further emphasized in the letter that the money should be spent for the good of human beings and not merely to bribe the agents of God. Expressing his anguish Tagore wrote, 'Sadly, such generous donors are reluctant to contribute towards mass education or bringing medical relief to their countrymen; little do they realize that the pious offerings that they make to their gods are all in vain. In no other country will you find such lack of interest or apathy in one man about another.'

What Tagore noticed and felt ragged about more than one hundred years ago has turned even uglier now. Barring a few exceptions, little resources are spent to alleviate the suffering of the people – the best of the creations of God. This is true about most of the religions, where much time and resources are spent in bribing the so-called agents of God and also running down the rival faiths. Tagore was not partisan in his approach to God. His God was universal and cared about humanity, with no sectarian or preferred choices. For him and his religious faith, love and harmony were central. He spoke in one of his addresses in 1908 that 'regardless of whether or not we know of any other truth, there is one truth deeply embedded in our hearts which is that only in love are all conflicts and contestations resolved and harmonized'.[29] Many of his writings and discourses are replete with empathy and care for fellow humans, which for him was the ultimate faith in the Creator for whom no distinction mattered. In one of his classic novels *Gora*, the main protagonist Gora is an Irish foundling who was lost in the Mutiny turmoil of 1857. He is brought up in an orthodox Hindu family but later discovers that he actually belongs to an alien race, which compels him to declare that

> no, I am not a Hindu … From the north to the southern end of India all the temple doors are closed to me … I have been liberated today … I have become free to reach a great truth. Today I am an Indian. Within me there is no conflict between the Hindu, Muslim, Christian and such communities. Today I am part of every caste … Tell now how to worship that Maker who is worshipped by Hindus, Muslims, Christians, Brahmos, by all alike – that Maker whose temple door is not closed to any race, any man … He who is the maker of India.[30]

Here, through the words of Gora, Tagore expresses his own commitment to syncretic Indian civilization and also to his 'religion of man', which is above everything else. Tagore's religion was ensconced with spirituality and love above everything else. While in a stark contrast, most religions today have everything else except the above two traits, and whatever they actually have is so extraneous to most of the religions.

Ramin also takes up an important aspect of Tagore's intellectual concerns – his passion for dialogue of cultures. This feature remained the core of Tagore's poetry and prose and also his idea of civilization. In his 2007 essay on 'Tagore and the idea of Civilization', Ramin wrote that "for Tagore, Man begins his life with his brute nature; but deeper within him is a current of universal humanity, which subordinates the brute nature to what Tagore considered the truth of Man: the Universal Mind'.[31] When he stresses the significance of dialogue among cultures, he assumes that all cultures, either of the east or of the west, have immense potential to take humanity forward. Therefore, Tagore always believed in the union of the east and the west and attached a huge importance to the cooperation of cultures across the world. He did never subscribe to the view of Kipling when the latter said, 'Never the twain shall meet.'[32] Tagore was fully convinced that 'the west has met the east', and this 'momentous meeting of humanity ... must have in its heart some great emotional idea, generous and creative'.[33] It is interesting to note that Harald Hjarne, chairman of the Nobel Committee, in the 'Award Ceremony Speech' appreciated Tagore's poetry as 'truly universally human in character' and eloquently pointed out that 'the poet's motivation extends to the effort of reconciling two spheres of civilization widely separated, which above all is the characteristic mark of our present epoch and constitutes its most important task and problem'.[34]

Several years before the Nobel Prize happened, precisely in 1908, Tagore wrote that 'in recent times the British have come to occupy an important place in India's history. That is not an accident.' He continued further and even said that 'without this contact with the west, India would have remained incomplete'. Here Tagore is almost accepting the inevitability of historical progress, where many changes are not merely accidental. For him cultures grow through interaction with each other. He asserts in the same essay that 'Europe lighted her (India's) lamp; we have to light ours from that flame and set out once more on our journey along the paths of time'.[35] What Tagore says later is quite relevant in the presently ongoing regressive discourse where some of us, the politically powerful today, believe that India is culturally secure only by exclusion and not assimilation. Tagore is prophetic when he says, 'How can those who think they had attained their completeness in their ancestors and must insulate their beliefs and practices against the touch of modernism, have the urge to live in the present, or have any faith in the future?'[36] He was firmly of the view that 'one of the most potent sources of Hindu–Muslim conflict in India is that we know so little of each other. We live side by side and yet very often our worlds are entirely different.'[37] Tagore was conscious of the closing down of our windows to the outside breeze. Any such revulsion is harmful for us as a nation and, of course, for the world we live in. I would like to quote a longish passage that will be aptly representative of the times we are living in today, particularly our relentless efforts to eliminate many parts of our history which we have dubbed as extraneous. He wrote in 1908:

> The objective of Indian history is not to set up Hindu or some other dominance, but to secure a special kind of fulfilment for humanity, a level of perfection that must be a gain for all. In the course of this fulfilment, if Hindu, Muslim and the British have to submerge the aggressive parts of their individuality, it may be hurtful to their national pride but it will not be reckoned as a loss in the scales of truth and human rights.[38]

Tagore urged us to look at our past not as a culturally monolithic entity but as a world which was a palimpsest, constituting diverse religions, cultures and languages. And all in harmony with each other. Ramin emphasizes Tagore's passionate pleas for cultural pluralism when he says that 'although convinced that moral progress lies in the direction of an inter-cultural alliance, Tagore insisted that cross-cultural learning was not something to be found as an accomplished phenomenon waiting to be recognized, but as a permanent effort to rethink and recreate the idea of cultural pluralism.' Tagore could see that our heterogeneity had been our strength, and the diverse strains in our cultural mosaic have enriched us immensely. He just couldn't imagine the possibility of purity of culture, a possibility of any culture that has grown or prospered without sharing with others.

Ramin has a section devoted to Tagore's educational ideas, a vocation that kept Tagore intensely engaged all his life. His ideas on education were never as relevant as they are today when the very basics of his educational ideals are being negated, in schools as well as universities. He had some very strong and even unconventional views about the ways education should be imparted. He believed that the joyless education system, based on 'learning a few prescribed textbooks by heart, and acquiring a working knowledge of a few subjects instead of mastering them',[39] produces adults with poverty of minds. He also feels strongly about the language of instruction when he says, 'And where do we make our sons and daughters spend their childhood? Among the grammars and lexicons of a foreign language; and within the narrow confines of a schoolwork which is dull and cheerless, stale and unending.' Ramin begins this section with a quote from Tagore's another essay, 'A Poet's School', written in 1926, where the focus was essentially on imparting education amidst nature, which Tagore emphasizes through examples from the literary classics of the east as well as the west. In the Robinson Crusoe story in the article, Tagore is moved by the adventure of the story 'where the solitary man is face to face with solitary nature, coaxing her, co-operating with her, exploring her secrets, using all his faculties to win her help'. Tagore conceived an education system that would offer the individual the opportunity of the fullest self-development in harmony with nature and society.

Tagore believed that a child should be brought up at home as well as in the school as a human being. A rich parent's child does not bring with him anything that distinguishes him from the child of the poor.

He also believed that schools cannot be imposed on society from outside; rather they should be integrated entities. In an article 'The Problem of Education', he said that 'any new schools founded by us fulfil the following conditions: that their courses are both lively and varied, and nourish the heart as well as the intellect; that no disunity or discord disrupts the minds of our young'.[40] Are we anywhere close to the ideals Tagore envisaged for our future education system? No, not really; on the contrary, our education system is breeding and promoting social disunity and disruption of minds. Unfortunately the educational ideal today is commercial and divisive where human values have turned hopelessly redundant. Tagore's primary objective of education was to facilitate the meeting of minds and encourage dialogue across cultures, religions and regions. As I said above, we have sadly traversed a distance that takes us away from the moral and idealistic world of Rabindranath Tagore. The school and university he founded at Santiniketan, a few miles away from Calcutta, were aimed at his efforts to change minds. 'I merely started with this one simple idea that education should never be dissociated from life.'[41] His emphasis on the growth and cultivation of the mind through education is expressed in his oft-cited poem, which is truly Tagorean in spirit:

Where the mind is without fear and the head is held high
Where knowledge is free
... Where the clear stream of reason has not lost its way into the
Dreary sands of dead habit
Where the mind is led forward by thee into over-widening thought
And action-Into that heaven of freedom, my Father, let my country awake.[42]

Tagore focused on the state of the mind in everything he pursued, and education was for him the cultivation of the mind as well. For him 'India's aim in education is to enable this mind to fulfil its quest in its own individual way ... For this purpose the mind of India must become organised and self-aware; then only will it accept education from its teachers in the right spirit.'[43] For him education was a creative activity where intellectual exploration was central. He continues to affirm that 'education becomes natural and wholesome only when it is the fruit of a living and growing knowledge'. He stood for an education that touches all aspects of our life, economic, intellectual, aesthetic, social and spiritual and where schools are integral to society and not just extraneous interventions. Tagore was open to borrowing all the good features of any system in education or anything else in life, but this needed to be integrated, particularly in education, in an organic way. In Europe, he said, 'one common medium of mind connects their teachers and students in a relationship which is living and luminous … This organic unity of mind and life and culture has enabled them to absorb truth from all lands and from all times, making it an essential element in their own culture.'[44]

After the partition of Bengal in 1905, besides political and revolutionary upsurge against it, there was a national education movement, as well with the founding of the National Council of Education in 1906. Tagore did get involved in it, and he raised some pertinent questions regarding the objectives of education. He wrote that 'if someone replies "education will be imparted in a national way", then the question arises as to what is a "national" way in respect of education? The word "national" has not been defined precisely. What is national and what is not will be determined by different people according to their individual training, convenience, beliefs and prejudices.'[45] Tagore had the courage to raise such questions about 'national' education during the emerging nationalist phase. He could talk about the preciseness of the category and freedom of the people to define it. Is it that easy to raise such questions today?

Another key element of Tagore's educational vision was to take the young minds away from the disease of parochialism and narrow sectarian way of approaching the world as well as your own country. Santiniketan attracted students from many other parts of India – for example, Gujarat, Kerala, Punjab and, of course, the neighbouring provinces – imparting a flavour of the nation as a whole to her culture.[46] While touring the United States in 1917, Tagore wrote to his son Rathindra from Los Angeles that 'Santiniketan must become "a centre of human studies regardless of nationality" and geography and parochialism'.[47] While inaugurating the Visva-Bharati as a central university in 1951, Maulana Azad referred to the three words, *Shantam, Shivam, Advaitam*, that Gurudev used in the objectives of the university. Here, Maulana continued, 'we have a conception of God which rises above all narrow limitations of race, religion or creed.'[48] Maulana emphasized on another important objective of the Visva-Bharati that Gurudev used in inaugurating all ceremonial functions of the university. It read, *Yatra Visyam Bhavatyekaneedam* (the whole world has here become one home).[49] Maulana expressed the desire that the university will continue with this appeal before all its programmes to express its faith in the unity of mankind. Unfortunately, these Tagorean ideals still remain relevant and elusive in our education as well as in our lives.

For Tagore, education has to be in sync with the needs of the times. He was categorical when he said that 'education in the modern age should be in harmony with the spirit of the times. Worshippers of nationalism consider it their duty to invent excuses for disseminating self-aggrandisement through education.' He also commented on how Germany has enslaved education to political animosities, and even other European nations, who are critical of Germany, have done that before. 'They have all used education as an incubator for hatching nationalism, with the difference that Germany being the most scientific of all has invented the best machine and hatched the best chicks. And what do their newspapers do but dish up lies with the same motive?'[50] These Tagorean words sound quite prophetic when we read them in the context of our ongoing educational changes that are peppered with a brand of narrow nationalism and are being implemented at school as well as university levels. The broad humanitarian vision of Tagore had no place for homogeneity. It was heterogeneity that was seen as the central pillar of education. While today, the exclusivist agenda reigns supreme, where most of the educational changes appear blatantly divisive.

Rabindranath Tagore's faith in the rational and scientific approach to life and its understanding had a tremendous bearing on the education system he conceived. He was a poet who, like all poets do, thrived on imagination, yet he shared deep bonds with scientists like Albert Einstein, whom he met five times. He also had a close relationship with the physicist Jagadish Chandra Bose and the statistician Prasanta Chandra Mahalanobis. He even authored a slim, little-known book, *Viswa Parichay*, which has allusions to gravitation and electromagnetism.[51] He begins the work, in a long dedication to his young friend the physicist Satyendra Nath Bose (known as the co-author of the Bose–Einstein statistics), with the remark that the Indian mind was yet to internalize the scientific attitude:

> In the forest leaves fall from the trees and that fertilizes the soil. In countries where science is cultivated little bits of that knowledge are spreading all the time. That fertilizes and animates a scientific mind. In the absence of that our mind remains unscientific. It is a poverty in the domain of knowledge as well as all the areas of our life and work.[52]

Tagore was taught astronomy by his father and learnt a lot through his readings of popular science which was surely not education in science, but it did help develop an awareness of science and 'an ability to see through the stupidity of blind faith'.[53]As a matter of fact, a scientific and rational attitude is not dependent on your study of science. It is a state of mind and Tagore stressed on its cultivation.

Besides his association with science and scientists, he repeatedly stressed on the cultivation of the mind when he wrote in 1921:

> The men who have released the human mind from the grip of the supernatural and the occult should all be acclaimed as masters, irrespective of whether they are Europeans or Asians.[54]

Tagore realized in this conflict between the east and the west that something has really gone wrong that has pushed us behind in the pursuit of scientific excellence. 'In these circumstances', he wrote in 1921, 'it will not help us in the East to condemn the learning which has enabled the West to conquer the world. Learning is truth, and by condemning it we shall only be condemning ourselves'.[55] His idea of education was centred around the ability to question, and he wrote that only 'animals live without conscious design, accepting events without question. To question events is the activity of man's highest nature and it shows that, unlike animals, man is a rebel.'[56] As in everything else, in education also Tagore stressed on the ability of the mind, a human being's faith in himself or herself and not really on chance as the core of intellectual prowess. He said about such people that 'not trusting their own intelligence, they give up questioning and cease to investigate. Looking for a Master outside themselves, they accept the power of anybody or anything, a policeman or a mosquito. Intellectual cowardice is the mainstay of weakness.'[57]

One of the most important chapters that Ramin includes in his book is 'The crisis in civilization and nationalism'. I say this because it was courageous of Tagore to write about it in the early-twentieth century, and it is not easy to critically engage with it now. It was a difficult task to talk about a cosmopolitan vision in the early-twentieth century, when nationalisms everywhere were xenophobic and aggressive.[58] The European nations were intoxicated with it, which finally culminated in the First World War. We in India were not very different. Our anti-colonial sentiment led some of us to a disdainful attitude towards anything foreign. Several revivalist movements in India had essentialized nationalism as Hindu or Islamic. In this milieu, it was difficult to hold a contrarian view.

It was Tagore who dared to question it and formulate a humanist vision, castigating the parochial and the bigoted. Sugata Bose, historian and a former member of the Indian Parliament, said in the House in a discussion on nationalism that 'I sometimes fear that those who are defining nationalism so narrowly will end up one day describing Rabindranath Tagore as anti-national if they read some of the sentences in his book on nationalism'.[59] This looks like a genuine possibility, given the combative attitude of many, sanctified by the state. Rabindranath Tagore's family was among the earliest Brahmos, as his grandfather was a close associate of Rammohun Roy. Rabindranath did go to school in India and England, but most of his education took place at home. He extensively travelled all over the world – maybe he was the most widely travelled Indian of his age. His understanding of the world, particularly of the emerging nationalism in Europe as well as Asia, was more nuanced than anyone else's. He could see the darker side of nationalism, which stifled the innate and instinctive qualities of the human individual and its overemphasis on the commercial and political aspects, at the expense of man's moral and spiritual qualities. When he was almost eighty, he could insightfully concede that 'lost in the glamorous aspects of British culture, I had never thought that, out of it come so cruel a distortion of long cherished values; that distortion, I knew at last, was the emblem of a civilized nation's contempt and callousness towards our vast masses'.[60] Tagore emphasized the humanitarian intervention into the self-seeking and belligerent nationalism, through the introduction of a moral and spiritual dimension. His internationalist and cosmopolitan vision was contrary to the narrow sectarian nationalism being espoused by nations across Europe and Asia.

Rabindranath Tagore, as I said above, had a much broader understanding of nationalism, which went beyond the idea of freedom from colonial subjugation or mere political freedom. He wrote about 'those of us in India who have come under the delusion that mere political freedom will make us free have accepted their lessons from the West as the gospel truth and lost their faith in humanity'.[61] His nationalism was more concerned with our age-old social inequalities, our hatred for each other in the name of caste, race and religion. He questioned the nationalism of our nationalists when he said that 'the very people who are upholding these ideals are themselves the most conservative in their social practice'. For Tagore, it was humanity above everything else, including nationalism, that also in the times when it was not easy to be so radically critical of the idea. While writing about nationalism and nationalists of his time, he stressed on the divisive social structure, a structure set up with boundaries of immovable walls to avoid collisions, 'thus giving to her numerous races the negative benefit of peace and order but not the positive opportunity of expansion and movement'.

Thus, it's a refreshing change of perspective and vision as we read Ramin engaging with nationalism and cosmopolitanism, focusing on Gurudev Tagore's disenchantment with the growing menace of jingoistic nationalism. Tagore penned a poem *The Sunset of the Century* on the last day of the nineteenth century, expressing both anguish and hope. He wrote:

> *The last sun of the century sets amidst the blood-red clouds of the West and the whirlwind of hatred.*
>
> *The naked passion of the self-love of Nations, in its drunken delirium of greed, is dancing to the clash of steel and howling verses of vengeance.*
>
> *The hungry self of the Nation shall burst in a violence of fury from its shameless feeding. For it has made the world its food.*
>
> *And licking it, crunching it and swallowing it in big morsels,*
>
> *It swells and swells*
>
> *Till in the midst of its unholy feast descends the sudden shaft of heaven piercing its heart of grossness.*[62]

As I said above, at the turn of the last century, Rabindranath Tagore saw nationalism as a source of misery, destruction and hate among people. This sentiment of the poet is expressed in many of his writings and letters and more particularly in three of his political novels: *Gora*, *Ghaire Baire* and *Char Adhyay*. He could foresee the consequences of this emerging madness, which ultimately led to the First World War, dividing and destroying nations. He stood for a dialogical world and hated the nationalism of Realpolitik and hyper-nationalism that breathed meaning into Thucydides's ancient maxim that 'large nations do what they wish, while small nations accept what they must'. He was appalled and shaken by the hardening of religious, national and linguistic identities. After the publication of his 1915 *Ghaire Baire* (*The Home and the World*), he was dismissed and mocked by many in the west, which included Marxist critics like Georg Lukacs and the English writer D. H. Lawrence. However, despite the derogatory condemnation of men like Lukacs and Lawrence, and the dismissal of him as a sentimental alarmist by others, Tagore's denunciation of nationalism proved prophetic with the outbreak of two world wars, causing huge loss of life and property. In his 1917 essay on nationalism, Tagore expresses his disenchantment with the pride and arrogance being promoted in Europe, when he says

> pride in every form breeds blindness at the end. Like all artificial stimulants its first effect is a heightening of consciousness, and then with the increasing dose it muddles it and brings an exultation that is misleading. Europe has gradually grown hardened in her pride in all her outer and inner habits. She not only cannot forget that she is Western, but she takes every opportunity to hurl this fact against others to humiliate them.[63]

Later in his life, Tagore is even more scathing in his critique when he writes that

> here in India the calamity of civilized rule is apparent not only in the grievous lack of the bare necessaries of life – food, clothing, educational and medical facilities – but even more deplorably in the way the nation has been split, divided against itself. To make matters worse, our social conditions alone are held in blame for the wretched state of affairs, even though this evil could not have taken shape without secret support from the topmost level in the administration.[64]

In the same essay he critically comments about India as well, and his words appear like a forewarning when he says that

> India has never had a real sense of nationalism. Even though from childhood I had been taught that idolatry of the Nation is

> almost better than reverence for God – and humanity, I believe I have outgrown that teaching, and it is my conviction that my countrymen will truly gain their India by fighting against the education which teaches them that a country is greater than the ideals of humanity.[65]

Tagore has left behind much that can help us understand the worth of the past. In the same essay on 'Nationalism', he continues that 'Europe has her past. Europe's strength therefore lies in her history. We, in India, must make up our minds that we cannot borrow other people's history, and that if we stifle our own we are committing suicide. When you borrow things that do not belong to your life, they only serve to crush your life.' In times when history is being rewritten, almost at all levels, we need to be conscious that blind nationalism will only add to our misery, and meddling with the past with a sectarian perspective will be a disaster. For Tagore, 'India is too vast in its area and too diverse in its races. It is many countries packed in one geographical receptacle.'[66] The attempts to see India as a homogenous entity are not just ahistorical; they are also antithetical to the very idea of India that was cherished and conceived by scholars, poets and visionaries like Tagore.

This deep and ugly divide is unfortunately being promoted by the state itself and not just by jingoistic groups. It has become an instrument to legitimately divide citizens of the same sovereign nation. The ugliest form of this so-called pride can be seen in Islam, which has been transformed into a reductionist political ideology, creating new adversaries. The xenophobic 'Islamic State' promises a nation clothed in a vulgarized Islam of their imagination. Today, we also witness 'Nation First' as a legitimate and respectable slogan, which resounds from India to the United States of America. Tagore appears to be a hardcore pragmatist, given all his misgivings about aggressive nationalism, and not a romantic, as some went on to call him.

Ramin moves to the comparative study of two important contemporaries, Rabindranath Tagore and Mahatma Gandhi. Both of them met first in 1915, through C. F. Andrews, soon after Gandhi arrived from South Africa. It was a meeting that unleashed a huge turmoil in the minds of both as they grew fond of each other yet also intensely disagreed on diverse issues. Gurudev was a multitalented man, committed to art, aesthetics, poetry and prose, painting and education and, of course, politics. Gandhi was essentially a political thinker and a man of action. I want to recall the words of Jawaharlal Nehru, who said in his message on the first death anniversary of Tagore on 7 August 1941:

> Tagore and Gandhi, each in his different way, was a symbol of India, steeped in her ancient culture and drawing strength and sustenance from her. How typical they were of India, and yet how utterly different from each other! Possibly no other country could have produced them, and they had their roots deep down in the Indian soil and their minds roamed over the many thousands of years that have gone to make India what she is … Both of them, in their respective and wholly different ways, represented that wonderful continuity of India's cultural tradition which has known no break though disaster has so often laid her low.[67]

No one could describe the two giants in a way Nehru could. He was intimately connected with both and had the capacity to read their minds. Both Tagore and Gandhi were deeply rooted in the soil of the country, yet they perceived their country and its problems so differently. They publicly differed and disagreed on many issues, yet it was Tagore who called Gandhi Mahatma, 'Great Soul', he said of him:

> He stopped at the thresholds of the huts of the thousands of dispossessed, dressed like one of their own. He spoke to them in their own language. Here was a living truth at last, and not only quotations from books. For this reason the Mahatma, the name given to him by the people of India, is his real name. Who else has

> felt like him that all Indians are his own flesh and blood? When love came to the door of India, that door was opened wide. At Gandhi's call India blossomed forth to new greatness, just as once before, in earlier times, when Buddha proclaimed the truth of fellow-feeling and compassion among all living creatures.[68]

Tagore was no different on this count, except that he impacted the minds of innumerable people while Gandhi worked on the flesh and blood. 'He too stopped at the thresholds of thousands, thousands of minds, not just in India but worldwide, and entered them.'[69] Gandhi recognized Tagore's worth and responded by calling him Tagore the Great Sentinel. 'I regard the Poet', he said, 'as a sentinel warning us against the approach of enemies called Bigotry, Lethargy, Intolerance, Inertia and other members of that brood'.[70] This warning against the evils mentioned above came from both of them, and it was never so pertinent as it is today. They did differ on several vital issues but stood together when it came to the fight against hate and bigotry. This makes both of them so relevant today. We need to remember them in action and not merely through lip service that we indulge in most of the time.

Tagore and Gandhi had different approaches in their engagement with science and technology. For example, Tagore intensely disagreed with Gandhi on his divine retribution remark on the 1934 Bihar earthquake. Tagore, on the other hand, did not see any divine intervention in physical phenomena. Again, both of them had open disagreements on the efficacy of charkha, where Tagore believed that 'the gifts of modern technology or science must not be judged by criteria which are irrational or alien to science'.[71] Tagore did not believe in dragging morality into matters of science, which, for him, should be handled through the test of reason. For Gandhi, morality and ethics were central even to visitations like droughts, floods and earthquakes.

Tagore and Gandhi took different positions on even the non-cooperation movement, particularly on the call to boycott the government educational institutions. Tagore seemed to take a more pragmatic view. He stressed on the loss of the youth who did not have enough national educational institutions to opt for, in which case their future will be at stake. Many of them did come back to the government colleges. For Gandhi, such calls were symbolic of a larger fight against colonialism and for freedom. For him, it was indispensable to make such sacrifices for a nobler objective. Tagore also disagreed with the ritual of burning foreign cloth unless cheaper cloth was available to the poor; 'he also questioned the economic rationale of depending on the charkha as the panacea when the issue was to build industry with ability to compete.'[72] However, Gandhi did respond to most of the apprehensions of the poet, mainly in *Harijan*, which he edited, and was quite precise and clear in his defence of all his political programmes. A good deal of what Tagore said, Gandhi believed, was said under 'poetic licence' and not to be taken seriously.[73] Responding on charkha, Gandhi said that he had only recommended spinning for half an hour on the charkha to those who were otherwise employed. For Gandhi, this was not merely an economic message but an ethical one and Gandhi did not draw a sharp distinction between economics and ethics. Tagore was bitterly criticized for his views against Gandhian programmes, and some of the nationalists went so far as to say that Tagore would have been guilty of treason had India been independent.[74] However, we need to remember that Tagore was scathing in his criticism of the west as well and never lost his ultimate faith in man. 'Even while he criticized the Mahatma, he recognized his greatness as a human being.'[75]

Tagore had deep faith in Gandhi's political sagacity. 'Gandhi's genius is essentially practical, which means his practice is immeasurably superior to his theory', he said later; as his plans worked out in practice, one realized 'the genius of this practical sage whose deeds surpass his words.'[76] In his article 'The Cult of the Charkha', Tagore wrote in 1925 that 'nothing is more wonderful to me than Mahatmaji's great moral personality'.[77] Gandhi likewise admired Tagore as a man of ideas. 'The poet lives in a magnificent world of his own creation – his world of ideas.' Gandhi generously allowed for Tagore's individual point of view, for 'our friendship becomes all the richer for our disagreements'.[78] Despite the feeling of revulsion among Gandhians and nationalists for some of the strong views of Tagore, their relationship remained cordial and respectful of each other in spite of political and other ideological differences.

VI

Ramin has dealt with some of those contributions of Tagore that are essential to remember today, not only in Bengal or India but also across the world. Tagore, as Ramin rightly says, was not a trained and organized philosopher, like so many of his contemporaries, but he was surely a sensitive soul who 'represented a nobility of spirit that not everybody in India could attain'. Tagore always had humanity in mind. In whatever he wrote or did, he never saw himself bound by any of the sectarian limits. In a world plagued with hate and divisive politics, the philosophy of Tagore has acquired salience that it never had ever before. We can see the tragic loss of Tagore's humanity in the ongoing deadly conflict in Gaza, where the weakest among the humans – women and children – are the worst sufferers.

Tagore lived through the period when nationalism and the politics of identity were at peak, and he decided to confront them head-on. Sadly, many in his own country have moved away from the human values that Tagore espoused all his life, and nationalism has become an instrument of passing judgement about our own fellow citizens. His faith in mankind and India's diversity appears to be the most dispensable idea today. It is not even seen as a virtue or strength but only as a source of weakness. His philosophy was rooted in the integration of humanity beyond national, ethnic, religious or racial identity. Sadly, all such identities are the most pronounced ones all across the world.

While concluding his philosophy of Rabindranath Tagore, Ramin comes back to the fetishized image of Tagore, created and sustained over the past few decades by the Bengalis, who revere him for his poetry and music. Of course, his contributions to art, poetry and music are seminal, but they should not be celebrated by an amnesia that ignores his philosophy of education and life in general. Besides being a poet of renown, Tagore had many very intelligible contributions. Ian Jack, writing on Tagore's 150th birth anniversary, commented, 'These are many. He was a fine essayist; an educationist who founded a university; an opponent of the terrorism that then plagued Bengal; a secularist amid religious divisions; an agricultural improver and ecologist; a critical nationalist.'[79]

Tagore's educational philosophy was a creative intervention in the conventional discourse of education in his times.[80] Ramin emphasizes that 'Tagore was against the idea of brainwashing children's mind through education. He believed that the continuous growth of the mind of the child should take place in a natural environment.' Like several other prominent educators of the world, Tagore also did not believe in imparting education through textbooks alone.

Tagore imagined a model of education that was based on the proper attention to the development and refinement of emotions, where diverse forms of art had a central place. He believed then, and it is even more true today, that societies are riven with hundreds of conflicts because the arts have been divorced from intimate contact with life. The university Tagore founded also stressed on his faith in the universality of human civilization, which is reflected in the founding ideals of the Visva-Bharati, where Tagore declared that 'though this

Visva-Bharati is India's own, it must become the site of the entire world's endeavour to not only disseminate but generate knowledge.'[81]

One of the most important messages left behind by Rabindranath Tagore is to go beyond an insular world and imbibe anything good from wherever you can, in any sphere from culture, and science to education. He wrote in 1933 that 'receptive minds must absorb the richness of new thought; the cross-currents of give-and-take flow fast at the points where the intellect is alive and awake.'[82] Any claim to become a *vishva guru* (world teacher) sounds hollow if we do not acknowledge what we imbibe from others and only stress on what we give to the world to enrich it. Tagore knew well that we live in a porous world where the flow of knowledge and culture is a two-way process.

This little book by Ramin does take care of many aspects of Tagore's life that are mostly not in circulation among the Tagore lovers. This does not mean that they have not been talked about, yet we need to imbibe his cosmopolitanism, particularly when narrow sectarian identities reign supreme. One of the most relevant and bold intervention of Tagore was his critical engagement with nationalism and Ramin comments in the conclusion that 'the rise of nationalism and sectarianism had led to a clash of fraternities, followed by the eclipse of human civilisation. Rabindranath Tagore, thus, became the geographer of the human soul, torn between empathy and revolt. For this pilgrim of the human soul, brotherhood alone could answer for evil and restore the spirit of humanity to its nobility.'

Introduction: Tagore, Our Contemporary

Rabindranath Tagore remains one of the most famous writers and inspiring thinkers of the twentieth century. As a creative writer and a spiritual guru, Tagore was in dialogue with the cultural and religious traditions of the east, while enriching himself with the humanist mind of the west. Tagore, however, in the judgement of many around the world, including some Indians, remains essentially a Bengali poet and educator. Yet, if an educator of any sort, Tagore is first and foremost the educator of humanity in general, and, as a poet, he has left us traces of his grandeur and nobility of spirit. As such, Tagore is not only a literary and philosophical figure; he is an idea and an inspiration for us and for generations to come. Maybe this is the reason why many philosophers, literary critics and historians of ideas are still drawn to study different aspects of Tagore's thought. As Mohammad A. Quayum argues, the principal reason for this is that

> Tagore wrote many of the sociocultural and political issues that are still pertinent to the present time. For example, he wrote on women's oppression and empowerment, the toxic effect of religious formalism, the importance of education, human dignity, environmental awareness, reason and freedom, the need for scientific and technological development, modernisation, equal rights for all citizens, cultivation of fellowship and respect across race and religion, egalitarian relations among cultures and countries, the horror of violence and war and the necessity for establishing world peace.[1]

Assuredly, Rabindranath Tagore is our contemporary, since we continue to relate to his thoughts, especially when engaging with a creative combination of spirituality, aesthetics and cosmopolitanism. According to Quayum,

> Tagore was not interested in any such political cosmopolitanism that would transform the Empire into a gigantic nation, in which the individual would still have to sacrifice his/her moral qualities for some political and commercial gain and surrender his/her spontaneous self to a virulent self-seeking and artificial life, which would bring power and prosperity but no inner fulfilment or lasting peace. Tagore's cosmopolitanism was more cultural and spiritual in nature, in which the individual would be expected to share a sense of hospitality and sympathy towards all fellow human beings.[2]

In other words, Tagore's philosophy had an ethical foundation which ultimately found its roots in his affirmation of the world. 'This world is not the creation of the Devil', wrote Tagore in a letter to Hemantabala Devi in October 1935,

> nor is it something that I have personally created. It is part of that Truth in which you seek the Transcendent. Spiritual life is affected when a part of that Truth is denied because of blind faith or out of a sense of pure revulsion. Our spiritual life becomes tainted when there begins to appear within its vanity, superstition, or irrational beliefs. This world turns holy when I begin to see in it the Bliss of Divine Presence … Do not doubt this world, do not hate it. He has not compromised His own Truth by creating a heaven apart from earth. Find happiness in everything; take it upon yourself to spread happiness among all. This alone will bring you salvation.[3]

Tagore seems to have been attracted more to spirituality rather than theology in different periods of his life. If anything, his philosophical strive was to further enquire about the spiritual potential in human beings. This leaves us arguing that Tagore, at different stages of his life, continued his quest for the sacred, combining a deep-seated approach to humanistic values with an intense love of the world. As Amiya Sen affirms, 'Man is the only being, as Tagore observed elsewhere, who was never fully reconciled to his status quo and that conflicts and contradictions only brought out the best in him. Religion, in this sense, was man's desire to be freed from the limitation of what is.'[4] It may be reasonably claimed that for Tagore the world, with its Truth and Beauty, is the greatest source of moral and spiritual fulfilment. In that sense, Tagore considers the world as a place of maturation and enlightenment for human beings. More than any of our contemporaries, Tagore seems to glorify the sense of revolt in Man. He writes in his famous poem, *Fireflies*: 'God honoured me with his fight when I was rebellious, he ignored me when languid.'[5] Tagore's humanism, in this sense, is about Man's effort to surpass the limitation of reality. Therefore, for Tagore philosophy is freedom of thinking and spiritual emancipation. It combines a deep-seated quest for Truth with an intensive love for Beauty. With Tagore,

> regardless of whether or not we know of any other truth, there is only one truth deeply embedded in our hearts which is that only in love are all conflicts and contestations resolved and harmonized. Differences in the realm of knowledge lead to heated arguments; in the realm of everyday activity, opposing forces keep fighting one another without yielding any ground. It is only in love that all conflicts are amicably resolved.[6]

An approach that Rabindranath consistently underlines here is to invite humanity not only to manifest its differences but also to surpass them. Accordingly, his vivid affirmation of life is fundamentally shaped by the concept of 'harmony'. For Tagore, the individual and the universal are both related to a non-static contemplation of life. Therefore, the fact that life develops infinitely and is ever perfected brings Tagore to conclude that wisdom suggests no indifference and passivity. As someone who takes the world to be dominated by reality and not by illusion (Maya), Tagore gives great importance to human agency and the quest for self-affirmation and self-respect as a quest for the basis of unity with the world. To Tagore, there was no question, therefore, of separating cultures, by simply asserting the superiority of the one over the other. Tagore was not the least hesitant in pointing out to the peoples of all cultures and civilizations the great menace of chauvinistic and sectarian views, which he found catastrophic for any form of universal coexistence and cooperation. Tagore was a cultural cosmopolitan but not a cosmopolitan in today's 'internationalist' sense. Thus, the fundamental conviction of Tagorean cosmopolitanism was that a practice of cultural pluralism is brought down directly to the individual and founded on ethical humanism.

It would be difficult to engage with Tagore's cosmopolitan outlook without taking into account Martha Nussbaum's inspirational work on this subject. Nussbaum makes a connection between Tagore's critique of nationalism and his cosmopolitan commitment to world citizenship. However, we can also add to Nussbaum's affirmation that Tagore's approach to cosmopolitanism is neither of a Kantian type, in reference to a philosophical-historical conception of universal reason, nor the celebration of a stoic kind of universal brotherhood. Also considering Tagore's philosophy of education in relation to his cosmopolitan rejection of nationalism, it seems more exact to talk about his idea of pedagogy as an empathetic form of humanism. Describing Tagore's educational work at Santiniketan, Nussbaum underlines:

> The school's pedagogy was primarily Socratic: teachers elicited answers by posing questions, rather than by lecturing; students even initiated the planning of the day's schedule. Classes were usually held outdoors, in close proximity to nature's beauty, so that the senses would be keenly receptive to beauty throughout the process. Above all, Tagore relied on the arts as key vehicles of development … The type of passionate humanism on offer at Santiniketan

> formed a certain sort of citizen, strong and unsubmissive, full of challenges to dead traditions. The link between Socratic inquiry and the arts made the critical spirit alluring.[7]

Tagore's cosmopolitanism was concentrated on his quest for freedom and empathetic pluralism as a shelter for human morality and politics. As such, Martha Nussbaum is correct to say that 'Tagore was both an individualist and a humanist. Although he disliked the idea of a world of uniform culture and values, he also saw moral ideals as fully universal, transcending ethnic, religious, and national differences.'[8]

Undoubtedly, if Tagore lived among us today, he would have rejected the cynicism and hypocrisy of what has come to be called the economic and political process of 'globalization'. For him, there would have been no true intercultural coexistence without a moral culture of brotherhood. Therefore, true globalization for Tagore should have been a moral and spiritual process, privileging the perpetual unfolding of human consciousness and helping the intellectual growth and moral maturity of mankind. Let us not forget that Tagore considered the denial of moral laws in the name of progress as one of the chief reasons for the chaos prevalent in modern civilization. Unlike 'globalization', Tagore's universal harmony integrated many opposites. As Satish C. Aikant underlines, Tagore 'saw no difference between the best ages of the past and present, east and west, there was no reason why a balance could not be achieved between the modern and traditional, foreign and native, religion and science, elites and masses, particular and universal. It is such balance between divergent strands that Tagore hoped to achieve in his universal worldview.'[9] As a matter of fact, Tagore remained deeply committed to a dialogical attitude in culture, education and spirituality, which rejected all forms of cultural and nationalist protectionism and exclusion of the other. However, he did not find the awareness and guidance he needed for such an attitude in the modern materialistic and technological civilization, but from a pluralistic vision which did 'not see modernity and tradition as dichotomous but as a dynamic fusion'.[10] It is this fusion that Tagore considered as a universal wisdom of humanity and which is addressed to our century as the essence of his contemporaneity.

We shrink back from the Truth of Tagore, if we believe that our present can be non-Tagorean. Needless to say, philosophy, art, spirituality, science and education are the five essentials which are needed for any civilization, but what is most needed is a moral capital which these means are meant to serve. And this implies, above all, a Tagorean world view which relates indeed to the quest for Truth and Beauty and is perfected by an attitude of prudent contemplation of reality, during which 'a sense of solidarity and a meaningful connection with others in the world'[11] is established. If this Tagorean manner of looking at reality does not prevail, then the essential goal of human civilization is lost. Tagore himself draws our attention to this situation when he affirms,

> Every civilisation uses its cumulative experiences to construct its conception of an ideal man. Every part of a tree ranging from the roots to the branches has but one objective: to have its fruits bear the finest seeds. In other words, it tries to concentrate in the seeds its quintessence, its optimum strength, and quality. The same is the case with human society: the ideal man is expected to represent the highest manifestation of human powers and potentiality.[12]

In a nutshell, what Tagore is saying is that modern civilization has to open its doors to wisdom, which is the permanence and the quintessence. As such, to say that our political, economic and technological future is determined by wise individuals is neither an exaggeration nor a dream. Tagore was well aware of the emancipative essence of wisdom in both classical India and ancient Greece, but he referred to the Indian sage as the image of the ideal man. He affirmed:

> Who did India take for its ideal man out of a host of talented, knowledgeable, and valiant kings and emperors? ... They happened to be the sages. Who were these sages? They were men whose minds were fully satiated upon perceiving the Great Soul (*paramatman*) through Knowledge; comforted to find It located in their souls, dispassionate upon experiencing it in their heart, and at peace with themselves once they found It revealed in everyday life and activity.'[13]

We can assume that Tagore was familiar with the opinion of Amir Khusraw in *Nuh Sipihr* when he declared that 'the Brahman of India is such a learned man that, as far as knowledge and learning are concerned, he has far excelled Aristotle'.[14] Most probably, Tagore, as in the case of Alexander's contemporaries, believed that India had more to offer in the domain of religion and spirituality than ancient Greece. As Richard Stoneman emphasizes in his book *The Greek Experience of India: From Alexander to the Indo-Greeks*:

> The word "philosophy" was invented by a Greek, but Greeks were entranced by Indian philosophy from early times. Pythagoras, who has the credit for inventing the word, was said to have longed to go to India but never made it. Philosophy in the Greek sense was a great deal more than is connoted by today's academic discipline, concerned as it is with definitions and meaning. Philosophy, "the love of wisdom", was a guide to life, and could even be applied to the way of life that was informed by wisdom. That is what Pythagoras meant by his coinage of the word: a life determined by the search for true understanding; and that is what the Greeks in Alexander's entourage seem to have thought they found in the Indian philosophers they met.[15]

However difficult it would be for the twenty-first century to accept and apply the Tagorean perspective of the Indian sage as the representative of the ideal human being, conscious of the concept of 'unitive empathy', it appears that some agreement can be reached if we accept to consider Tagore himself as a writer–thinker who belongs to the Goethian idea of *Weltliteratur.* Tagore not only attempted to revive the concept of *Weltliteratur,* but also tried to re-elaborate this concept in the mirror of Indian spiritual tradition. One may be tempted to dismiss Tagore as an irrelevant and unrealistic thinker in the context of our global world. However, the truth is that Tagore's pluralistic approach, amplified by that of what we can call an empathetic diversity, makes him a strong pretender of an intercultural global world. The issue of intercultural dialogue occupied Rabindranath Tagore throughout his life. This interest is best indicated by the expression 'Unity in Diversity', which he often used in his essays and addresses. Throughout his life, he consistently opposed uniformity and contrasted it with the ideal of unity. True unity, Tagore believed, was only possible by celebrating diversity through a dialogue among cultures. The pursuit of harmony remained an ideal for Tagore beyond the imperatives of modernity as a way of relating various cultures and achieving unity in diversity.

If Tagore's philosophy is the outcome of the conflicts and aspirations in modern India, philosophy, in turn, is the moral standard by which he judges progress. Tagore was opposed to modern civilization for its lack of wholeness and its predilection for the material rather than the moral progress of humankind. Tagore had no illusion about what is called 'progress' and has come to be synonymous with the law of necessity rather than the law of truth. For Tagore, progress was the free expression of human personality in harmony with life. Therefore, the real crisis of modern civilization was due not to the conflict and clash between cultures but between Man and the idea of life as a whole. According to Tagore, the problem of Man lies to a great extent in his inability to relate to the idea of wholeness. His stress on emancipating human beings from the servitude of hugeness (an inspiration for Fritz Schumacher's *Small is Beautiful*) is related to his deep-set conviction that there is no inherent contradiction between the claims of the so-called opposites such as the human and the divine, Beauty and Truth, social responsibility and individual rights, respect for traditions and openness towards a new world and finally love of one's country and belief in the unity of mankind. For Tagore, these opposites can and must be reconciled, not by force and subjugation but by finding a true harmony among the apparent divergences.

Tagore was in search of common roots of human coexistence. However, this did not need to take the form of a single world religion, nor did it stand in need of older organized religions. What Tagore was after would be the 'Universal Man', which had a uniquely organic connection to reality and thus could provide a moral and aesthetic reflection of how the world was organized. 'Do not be misled into thinking that my spiritual objective is to focus on one particular personality through my meditation', he was to write, 'I only try to realize within me the Eternal and the Universal Man … In Europe, there are many atheists, who, by realizing the idea of the Universal Man, render their work glorious. Their concern is for all times and for people of all countries. Those who are obsessed with the need for ritual correctness end up venerating only themselves.'[16] Given this kaleidoscopic outlook, we can say that for Tagore the truth of Man is the unity and harmony in life. Maybe that is why, even at the moment of finishing his life's work, Tagore's life or life for Tagore never lost its meaning. He was responsible and empathetic in his journey across time, vouching for all the moments of his life. As a pilgrim, he would search for Truth, no matter where he lived, and yearned for a world where he could dwell with a whole harmonious humanity. Therefore, Tagore belonged to a generation of outstanding poets and thinkers who had a compulsion to search for the truthful and the beautiful. And maybe, that is why, far from being outmoded, Tagore is our contemporary. His powerful transcultural potential and his humanist approach to the idea of harmony and love are the foundations of the common humanity. 'Only with love', wrote Tagore, 'is it possible to bring about this out-of-the world experience whereby those, which, by their very nature were contradictory, lose all contradictions.'[17]

Tagore's life was blown about by the winds of the nineteenth and twentieth centuries. Therefore, it is impossible to understand his philosophical thoughts without understanding the events that shaped India and the world. However, there is more to Tagore's life than just minutes of a remarkable life lived during a fascinating century. If Tagore is our contemporary, it's because his life is of perennial importance, and his thoughts and writings ask for our philosophical meditations and reflections. These meditations and reflections need to be formulated in the same spirit of excellence and frankness that Tagore himself has championed in his approach to his life and writings. But it also needs to be a silent dialogue with Tagore himself. Tagore dreamt of culture under the banner of fraternity. This is a vision that is important to us today: to put Tagore, the intercultural Indian, at the service of the heritage of the nobility of the spirit. Let us stress that, for Tagore, interculturality cannot be reduced to a merely touristic conception of culture but rather is an intellectual and spiritual endeavour that presents itself as a major means for the aesthetic and moral education of humanity. In his metaphysical conception of humanity, Tagore places the crucial region of the human soul at the centre of his intercultural vision of the world. In truth, interculturality is not a way of imposing one's culture on others. We know that Tagore never sacrificed the Universal Man in the name of Indian nationalism. He, therefore, dismissed any form of nationalism, either eastern or western, as an ideal of selfishness that destroyed moral civilization. According to Satish Aikant,

> Tagore was passionately committed to the interaction of cultures, both from a normative conviction that universal Truth could only be revealed through the comparative study of cultures and from a historical appreciation of the inescapable hybridity of all cultures, including those of the Indian subcontinent. He was an insistent

> universalist in his belief that moral truth is one, indivisible and omnipresent; hence, any external organisational form that seeks to contradict that truth is a moral offence. According to Tagore, the idea of Indianness does not supersede the idea of Indian civilisational unity, which incorporates several divergent strands of national culture. The cosmopolitan universality envisioned by Tagore was premised on the belief that a culture could reflect universal ideas without a loss to national identity.'[18]

Thus, for Tagore, the deification of the nation created exclusivism, fanaticism and violence. In other words, according to Tagore, every nation considered the other as a threat to its existence and waged war against it for self-fulfilment. Moreover, Tagore, like Gandhi, saw modern civilization with its perpetual pursuit of wealth as an immoral and *adharmic* civilization. To Tagore, the Universal Man was at the centre as well as the circumference of life. Therefore, he saw modern civilization with its perpetual pursuit of wealth as a monstrosity of the nobility of spirit of mankind.

Perhaps Tagore's vision of an intercultural and multi-visionary humanity, free from the fetters of materialism, nationalism as well as religious and racial orthodoxy – actively seeking a common universal destiny and a shared spiritual fate – looks too sublime and unrealizable for our complacent and conformist world. However, this does not mean that we should stop reading Tagore and thinking with him about our present and future. Tagore's call for a dialogical exchange among cultures and religions beyond exclusivism, provincialism and fanaticism, where each culture is required to keep its independence while not forgetting its empathy, appears as a relevant solution to the problems of our decivilizing world. Contrary to the common perception, decivilization is not the absence of civilization; rather, it is a state of meaningless and thoughtless civilization. More than physical pain, a meaningless and thoughtless existence degrades humanity by robbing it of its self-esteem. A society may be said to be in a state of decivilization when its individuals are divested of their capacity for empathy as a tool for the recognition of the otherness of the Other. As such, what Tagore teaches us is that no civilization constitutes a hermetically sealed ensemble. The boundaries of a culture may change as it encounters other cultures. This is how it has been all through human history. In that case, Tagorean critical intercultural dialogue could lead to change where the process of dialogue and transvaluation of values replaces that of imitation, coercion or manipulation. When it is done in this manner, the partners in an intercultural dialogue end up engaging in a process of questioning rather than intimidating or patronizing each other.

What we can call the Tagorean moment of questioning unethical civilization refers not to Tagore's historical milieu but to a distinctive cultural experience of the human spirit. Accordingly, the creative-constructive side of Tagore's moral and educative philosophy points to an alternative notion of civilization. Tagore, next to Gandhi, is an intercultural Indian who redefines civilization as a moral compass and a space of dialogue. His analysis of interculturality helps to nurture a plural and cosmopolitan citizenship, but it also directly confronts the ecology of violence and moral incapacity for self-examination and self-realization in Indian society and the world. That is to say, for Tagore, understanding and respecting the otherness of the Other is more than a simple act of tolerance. It includes a move beyond the mental ghettos in which we imprison our minds. This in turn allows the creation of a space for creative questioning, which raises further questions about our ethical responsibilities to other parts of the collective to which we belong. We see here how the full understanding of the process of freedom-making necessitates for Tagore a civilizational acceptance of the Other as the Other. As a matter of fact, it comprises two major dimensions which are at the heart of Tagore's philosophy of respecting the otherness of the Other: a pluralistic and inclusive form of togetherness and interconnectedness among individuals and cultures and a creative inner freedom. This is where the Tagorean moment of questioning reality is always accompanied by an individual project of aesthetic creativity and inner freedom. It appears very clearly in the Gandhi–Tagore debate in *The Call of Truth* (1921), *The Cult of the Charka* (1925) and *Striving for Swaraj* (1925). According to Sir Richard Sorabji,

> Tagore and Gandhi seem to agree that there is a personal inner freedom and a freedom of the country, and that the inner freedom is the prior prerequisite. But freedom (swaraj) for Gandhi and Tagore is nonetheless very different. For Gandhi, freedom for the country is not merely home rule, rule by Indians, but home rule based on the inner freedom of self-rule for Indians as individuals. Otherwise, Indian rulers might suppress freedom as much as any others. The necessary inner self-rule can only be obtained by disciplines for reducing one's desires: the disciplines, so he wrote in 1909, of non-violence, supported by chastity, poverty, truth and fearlessness … Tagore agreed and disagreed. He agreed that alien government in India was a chameleon. It might be the British today, other foreigners another day, and, with no less virulence, Indians the next day. But he went further. Alien government is maya, illusion, and will vanish of itself, if we can gain within us the truth called our country. I suspect there is only an illusion of government because of the point noticed above in *Striving for Swaraj*, that a country is one's own only if one has helped to create it. Gaining within us the truth called our country, Tagore continues, requires something more positive than the disciplines of renouncing desires. It requires our inner faculties and forces. It requires something more positive also than Gandhi's proposal of noncooperation with the British. Moreover, the creation of one's country and its freedom calls, like yoga, for all the human powers and faculties, all the forces of the country, not just one exercise like spinning. The economist must think, the educationist and statesman must think and contrive. The country will not get freedom (swaraj) without intellect and will. The welfare of the people is a synthesis comprised of many

> elements. Health and work, wisdom, reason and joy must all be thrown into the crucible. The creation of the country requires all the varied powers of man along many and diverse roads.[19]

Tagore's debate with Gandhi shows us clearly his favourable attitude towards the concept of 'negative liberty' rather than 'positive liberty'. However, Tagore's inclination for the 'negative' freedom of the individual not to be interfered with, as a narrative of creativity and freedom with art and culture's moral and political functions, does not necessarily mean that the Tagorean moment of questioning reality is non-political. Assuredly, Tagore believes that the creative individual should be free of any external barriers or constraints. However, he also believes that the act of taking control over one's life and realizing it socially and politically is an important part of the creative life of the individual. Tagore always believed in the transformative role of creativity. For him, every individual had to cherish three kinds of freedom: freedom of mind, freedom of heart and freedom of will. According to him, this was the true message of modernity, different from any form of imitation of Europeans. This is what he wrote in his essay on 'Nationalism in Japan': 'One must bear in mind, that those who have the true modern spirit need not modernise … Modernism is not in the dress of the Europeans; or in the hideous structures … True modernism is freedom of mind, not slavery of taste. It is independence of thought and action, not tutelage under European schoolmasters.'[20] Tagore is well known for his aversion to the modern bureaucracy, where we can find the absence of individual creativity in concentrated and organized form. As such, individuality must always keep pace with creativity. In other words, Tagore's wager is that the aesthetic education of humanity can overcome the rule of mass production, while avoiding the pitfalls of authoritarianism. Truly, what is at stake here for Tagore is 'the promise of a possibility that has driven human civilization to go beyond its current state of existence, age after age … In our ordinary lives, the importance of happiness and unhappiness may be great, but this undergoes change once man goes beyond self-interest.'[21]

Tagore deliberately disassociated individual freedom and creativity from political independence. He, therefore, pointed to a deeper level of change, at times amounting to a radical appeal to the creative self. In other words, to Tagore, the moral claim to rule was nonsensical, even reckless, without a practical demonstration of individual creativity. He wrote:

> It is my belief that there might come the day when we shall become fully conscious of our own private worlds. At this stage, we see the many streams of consciousness in broken and fragmented forms and this renders it difficult to read any concrete meaning into our feelings and experiences. However, when such sundry experiences are suitably arranged, we would discover a glow even within that which appears grotesque and misshapen to the naked eye. At that auspicious hour, the vital, inner meaning of world-drama will reveal itself to me.[22]

Creativity was, of course, for Tagore, a form of living, a source of catharsis and wisdom. Of course, Tagore always lived ahead of himself. His actuality and contemporaneity, then, extend beyond his death.

This book envisages two audiences. The first is a general learned audience, namely all those who want to know more about the first Asian Nobel Prize winner in literature and become with the ideas of an intercultural philosopher and poet. However, at the same time, the book casts university students and those intrigued by the South Asian history of ideas. Not surprisingly, the main ones are interculturality and critique of fanaticism. The thought and philosophy of Rabindranath Tagore is the focus of five chapters. Chapter 1 profiles Tagore's ideas of God and Nature and their significance for Man. Man is seen by Tagore as a conscious being and God as a supreme consciousness. When Tagore talks about Man, he is not referring to an everyday living being, but to a creative human life that advances from quantity to quality. Therefore, Man is a self-conscious and self-interpreting creature who advances and changes in the direction of intellectual and spiritual maturity. This, of course, begs the questions of culture and interculturality, which are discussed in Chapter 2. This chapter takes a specific look at Tagore's intercultural philosophy and his hopes for the victory of universal humanism for the victory of human solidarity against nationalism, sectarianism, communalism and religious fundamentalism. Joining the club of famous intercultural Indians like Ghalib and Dara Shikoh, Tagore looks at specific aspects of his Indianness as a capacity of understanding other cultures. This is a reminder of Tagore's educational awareness of intercultural dialogue as a unique way to understand and rediscover humanistic wisdom. By this point, the centre of gravity of the book will shift to the Tagorean approach to education. In Chapter 3, we will discuss the educational ideas of Tagore and his groundwork efforts for an international educational centre that would facilitate communication among cultures. Because Tagore saw life through an intercultural lens, he felt constantly the need to refer to the educational maturity and pedagogical awareness of humanity. Generally speaking, Tagore was an optimistic philosopher, but his last writings on the crisis of human civilization show a strong degree of cultural pessimism and political distress. As such, Chapter 4 will take a closer look at Tagore's rejection of the concept of nationalism in India and elsewhere by discussing at the same time his deep concern with the proto-totalitarian enslavement of human beings and their capacity to think. Though in opposition to the British Raj, Tagore found Indian patriotism dangerously vulnerable to the negative tendencies of nationalism. Tagore's intentions seemed very clear: as a colonized Indian, he sought to establish a bridge with western modernity without necessarily demonizing western civilization. Tagore's humanist view of nationhood came from the awareness that the idea of nation, nationality and nationalism were totally incongruent with Indian self-definition. However, the key point for Tagore in understanding Indianness was his extraordinary aesthetic and civic creativity that enabled him to keep himself rooted in Indian traditions while being open to the message of modernity. What was striking about Tagore was his progressive urge to rescue his countrymen from the imperative of unreason. He knew that everybody should cultivate the art of listening to modernity, especially all Indian leaders like Gandhi who were fighting against the British for the independence of India. This argument makes it easier to come to Chapter 5, a chapter which deals with the famous debate between Gandhi and Tagore. Both Tagore and Gandhi tried to have a rational and compassionate understanding of their common world. To be sure, what the conversations between the two men show us is a sense of urgency to understand the historical event in which they find themselves beyond its paradoxes and contradictions. This ability to experience the twentieth century without any bitterness for the cultural traditions of India helped Tagore to live the moments of ambiguity of the making of a new India with a secular orientation to life and a democratic view of the Indian society. This is what the reader can learn from the conclusion of this book, that Tagore was undoubtedly the restless genius who stood against the world where only the spirit of fanaticism remained. He was the conscience of a world where great civilizational changes were underway. Tagore was among those Indian intellectuals who championed the faculty of thinking critically in order to overcome the evils of his own socio-cultural milieu, while knowing well that freedom is not always born in blood and fire.

1

Man, God and Nature in Tagore's Philosophy

Holderlin's statement, 'Poetically, man dwells on this Earth', has relevance both to Tagore's idea of Man in general and to Tagore, the poet in particular. Truly speaking, Tagore's creative work, either as poetry or as essay, can be considered because of his experience of living on Earth. Tagore's sense of residing on Earth is represented by his metaphysical vicinity with the three concepts of Man, God and Nature. Tagore does not only celebrate the majesty and infiniteness of God but also talks about his created world and Nature and his relation with Man. 'Tagore lays focus upon realization of God in the heart of humanity and puts stress on the essential unity of man, God and Nature almost in all his poetical works. All discord and disharmony get resolved into unity and harmony.'[1] There is a certain vision of harmony and unity here that one can find in all Tagore's writings. As Sarvepalli Radhakrishnan rightly argues, 'Rabindranath uses the visible world as a means of shadowing forth the invisible. He touches the temporal with the light of the eternal.'[2]

Generally speaking, there are two levels in Tagore's idea of religion: the universal level and the individual level. He points out in his Hibbert Lectures at Oxford in March 1930: 'My religion is in the reconciliation of the super-personal man, the universal human spirit, in my own individual being.'[3] A closer look at Tagore's spiritual philosophy reveals that, for him, Man is in existential despair without the help of a universal principle. However, a limited and finite God cannot assure a spiritual soul, since the opposition of good and evil will remain. Therefore, God gives birth to the universe as an Absolute since He is the foundation of the whole universe and the infinite expression of perfection. Rabindranath, therefore, admits that God is the foundation of the whole universe. According to Tagore, 'the revealment of the infinite in the finite, which is the motive of all creation, is not seen in its perfection in the starry heavens, in the beauty of the flowers. It is in the soul of man.'[4] In other words, Tagore's approach to religion is one definite way of arriving at fellowship with God. This connectedness is obviously of a poetic essence. He explains:

> My religion is essentially a poet's religion. Its touch comes to me through the same unseen and trackless channels as does the inspiration of my music. My religious life has followed the same mysterious line of growth as has my poetical life. Somehow, they are wedded to each other, and through their betrothal had a long period of ceremony, was kept secret from me.[5]

As such, Tagore saw the unity of existence as a matter of spiritual experience. Tagore's love of God is the result of his daily experimentation with art, literature and philosophy. This is done not by a theological approach to a God, whom Man fears and serves, but through union with a spirit that is everywhere. Tagore asserts: 'I felt that I had found my religion at last, the religion of Man, in which the infinite became defined in humanity and came close to me so as to need my love and cooperation.'[6] Tagore has the firm faith that there is an inseparable connection between God and Man. Thus, Man's life is blessed by the opportunity which has been given to him to experience the divine in all its aspects. Tagore observes the unity of Man and God in the wholeness of the world and our oneness with it. He declares: 'Man, as a creation, represent the Creator and this is why of all creatures it has been possible for him to comprehend this world in his knowledge and feeling and in his imagination to realise in his individual spirit a union with a spirit that is everywhere.'[7]

Of all creatures, Man is the only one who is conscious that God is universal love and radiant joy. That is why, he announces in *Gitanjali* (16) that 'I have had my invitation to this world's festival, and thus my life has been blessed. My eyes have seen and my ears have heard. It was my part at this feast to play upon my instrument, and I have done all I could.'[8] Tagore cries out the joy of the wholeness of his personal experience with the divine. Tagore often expands on the Upanishads in his writings and points out to the phrase *Advaitam is anandam*, the Infinite One is Infinite Love. Here lies Tagore's central idea that 'Man's religion is his innermost truth.'[9] Here, two things are to be noted. First, Man for Tagore is not merely coming from Him but is also going towards Him. Life must move on. Second, as long as life is not lived through love and with the consciousness of the infinite in Man, we are bound in the finite realm of Nature. We need, therefore, to express infinity in everything around us. According to Sarvepalli Radhakrishnan, explaining Tagore,

> life is a process of eternal birth and death. Birth is death, and death is birth. All progress is sacrifice. The finite self which has to be transformed into the infinite, which is its destiny, does not easily lend itself to this transformation. We have to lay violent hands on it before we can force it to express the infinite. So long as man is finite, the infinite within him tries to break through the finite. The spirit chafes against the bonds of the flesh. There is ever a striving forward in man to make real the infinite which he already is … Till therefore the infinite is reached, the life of the finite individual will be one of strenuous effort and untiring toil, involving risk and daring, strain and conflict … Struggle, therefore, is the world's supreme blessing. Man is born for it as he reaches his aim through it.[10]

The notion of struggle in Tagore is mostly *cathartic*, because it refers to the 'purification' of the self. There, we are not dealing with a Hegelian struggle for recognition between two self-conscious individuals in a relation of dependence. Radhakrishnan explains the Tagorean process by referring to *Svetasvatara Upanishad*. According to him,

> the infinite in man is like the oil in the sesamum seeds, or butter in curds, water in river, or fire in the two pieces of wood. To get oil from sesamum seeds we have to press them, churn the curds before we can have butter, dig the ground for water, and rub the sticks for fire. This is suffering or hardship. Till the goal of the infinite is attained we have risks and dangers. We have to fight with infinite, not physical wars, but spiritual wars. Every moment our finiteness is transcended.[11]

In a way, Tagore is inspired by the Upanishadic message of understanding the nature of the ultimate reality and having access to Universal Soul's nature. Further than the metaphysical content of this message, there is a strong dialogical essence to it. As it is observed by Kaylan Sen Gupta,

> in this way the *Upanishads* purport to highlight the central metaphysical truth about ourselves. Each of us is an expression of the Universal Soul, or, put differently, each of us is this same Soul or atman. Now if each of us belongs to the Universal Soul, if the same Infinite is equally present in all of us, then we ourselves are at bottom identical or one with each other. Recognition of this truth paves the way to our openness to others, and generates in us love and concern for our fellow beings.[12]

Life is seen by Tagore as a formation and a fulfilment. In this journey Man is a conscious being and God a supreme consciousness. What is expected of Man? To be a creative being and to manifest the Infinite in itself. So, Man needs God to be Infinite, but God also needs Man to be loved. In his book *The Gardener*, Tagore asks from God if this love is true: 'Tell me if this be all true my lover', writes Tagore, 'is it true that your love travelled alone through ages and worlds in search of me?'[13] What is so interesting and positive about Tagore is that his readings of the wastern and western civilizations, especially of India's heritage, is free of prejudice and a preconceived idea. As Sen Gupta underlines correctly,

> 'Tagore, then, had no dogmatic loyalty to the Upanishads; rather, he draws upon them in order to fashion his own account of human beings and their world. The Upanishadic concern was primarily the cognitive quest for an understanding of ultimate reality, from which there would then flow an account of human beings and their interrelationship. Tagore, however, does not commit himself to the particular doctrine of reality as an infinite spirit or World-Soul that was advanced in the Upanishads. In fact, he is suspicious of traditional metaphysical arguments for such a view.[14]

It is in Nature that Man has glimpses of God and the fullness of reality. Tagore's deep feeling for Nature is an expression of the unity of Man and God in the cosmic aspiration towards greater perfection. For Tagore, Man is in search of everlasting joy and rhythm in the stream of Nature. Therefore, the invitation is there – always and eternal – from the world of Nature to the world of Man. In other words, in Tagore's mind, the vision of Nature is an important component for the renewal of his vision of humanity. This is a vision from an outer dimension to an inner grandeur – the grandeur of serenity. In other words, in Tagore's mystical journey, to sit face to face with Nature is to be blessed with the prized moment of the All Beautiful. In the opinion of K. Krishnamoorthy, 'Perception of beauty according to Tagore is directly dependent on the degree of sensibility cultivated by man towards fellowmen and nature.'[15] That is to say,

> The chief obstacle in the way of man's realising beauty is said to lie in his self-centredness or egoism. True is that which, in one sweep, embraces the universal man; and the walls of egoism that rise between man and man only serve to shut out the glimpses of the all-pervading beauty in Man and Nature. Sensual beauty

> is thus to be distinguished clearly from spiritual beauty which is the law of life. The latter cannot be appreciated by one whose life is unrestrained. Sensual restraint, then, is the first and foremost requirement in the appreciation of genuine beauty.[16]

Tagore seems to be guided in all his different spiritual and artistic activities by a direct and unquestioning vision which leads him towards a philosophy of wholeness and unity. Maybe that is why Tagore all through his life kept up his interest in Nature. This is how he expresses his love of Nature in a letter written at the age of twenty-one:

> The more one lives alone on the river or in the open country, the clearer it becomes that nothing is more beautiful or great than to perform the ordinary duties of one's daily life simply and naturally. From the grass in the field to the stars in the sky, each one is doing just that; and there is such profound peace and surpassing beauty in nature because none of these tries forcibly to transgress its limitations.[17]

Tagore considers the aesthetic experience of Nature as a joy of empathy (what Herder calls *Einfühlung*), which consists of being lifted out of ourselves and being identified with the objects of Nature. But the aesthetic experience is not only an *outwardization* of the self, it is equally an *inwardization* of objects. 'This world which takes its form in the mould of Man's perception,' affirms Tagore in his book *Personality*, 'still remains as partial world of his senses and mind. It is like a guest and not like a kinsman. It becomes completely our own when it comes within the range of our emotions. With our love and hatred, pleasure and pain, fear and wonder continually working upon it, this world becomes a part of our personality.'[18] Tagore believes in the unity of the world, enriched by the immense diversity of its manifestations. For him, each human being has its own uniqueness and is at the same time a part of the divine personality. He believes in the perfect harmony which has ideal Beauty. And here Tagore joins Keats to say that Beauty is Truth and vice versa. Accordingly, in a conversation with Albert Einstein on 14 July 1930, Tagore describes the Truth of the universe as a human truth and he adds, 'Beauty is in the ideal of perfect harmony, which is in the Universal Being, truth the perfect comprehension of the universal mind. We individuals approach truth through our own mistakes and blunders, though our accumulated experiences, through our illumined consciousness.'[19]

According to Tagore, the essence of Man is the Infinite which is part of its essence. Therefore, its 'dharma' is to become the Infinite by breaking the limitations of its narrow selfhood and bringing itself in contact with Nature. As such, Man's deepest joy is in growing greater in terms of a profound union with Nature. 'When a Man does not realize his kinship with the world', underlines Tagore in his book *Sadhana*, 'he lives in a prison-house whose walls are alien to him. When he meets the eternal spirit in all objects, then he is emancipated, for then he discovers the fullest significance of the world into which he is born; then he finds himself in perfect truth, and his harmony with the All is established.'[20] As we can see, Tagore describes Nature primarily as a reservoir of peace to which humanity could be attached for regeneration. And since God is present in Nature, we ought to love Nature to fulfill and realize ourselves. Thus, love for God is translated into love for Nature. This world view in Tagore results from the Upanishadic idea of a living presence of God in all created objects. As a result, there is a sense of interconnectedness between the physical and the spiritual that espouses the visible and the invisible simultaneously. Thus, Tagore saw life as a continuous process of synthesis between the ideal and the real and between Beauty and harmony. As Tagore himself puts it,

> in the night we stumble over things and become acutely conscious of their individual separateness. But the day reveals the greater

> unity which embraces them. The man whose inner vision is bathed in an illumination of his consciousness … no longer awkwardly stumbles over individual facts of separateness in the human world, accepting them as final. He realizes that peace lies in harmony.[21]

As far as the relationship between Man and Nature is concerned, the latter is a sure refuge, so that Man can call out for its help. In the Man–Nature relationship, there is peace, calm and serenity. As Ezra Pound argues,

> there is in Tagore stillness of nature. The poems do not seem to have been produced by storm or by ignition but seem to show the normal habit of his mind. He is at one with nature and finds no contradictions. And this is in sharp contrast with the Western mode, where man must be shown attempting to master nature if we are to 'great drama'. It is in contrast to the Hellenic representation of man as the sport of the gods, and both in the grip of destiny.[22]

Despite its non-Hellenic essence, Tagore's poetry is deeply philosophical. Tagore's philosophy is not that of a system-builder but the philosophy of a poet. Poetry helped Tagore to bridge the gap between himself and reality and to enter more deeply into the mystery of the divine. In quest of his 'beloved', Tagore is waiting at God's door. He writes in *Gitanjali* (poem 41): 'I wait here weary hours spreading my offerings for thee, while passers by come and take my flowers, one by one, and my basket is nearly empty … Oh, how, indeed, could I tell them that for thee I wait, and that thou hast promised to come.'[23] Talking about Tagore, the poet–philosopher, we find in his philosophical poems and his poetic philosophy an ardent desire of a spiritual pilgrim who is seeking a total union with God and the world. His adoration of the Universal Man and of Nature, in his philosophical essays like *Sadhana*, *Personality* and *The Religion of Man*, echoes back his quest for unity and his hope of dwelling with God in *Gitanjali*. Tagore writes:

> The song that I came to sing remains unsung to this day. I have spent my days in stringing and in unstringing my instrument. The time has not come true, the words have not been rightly set; only there is the agony of wishing in my heart. The blossom has not opened; only the wind is sighing by. I have not seen his face, nor have I listened to his voice; only I have heard his gentle footsteps from the road before my house. The livelong day has passed in spreading his seat on the floor; but the lamp has not been lit and I cannot ask him into my house. I live in the hope of meeting with him; but this meeting is not yet.[24]

Tagore's despair is full of hope, since he knows that the Light will come and the darkness shall be dispelled. According to Jose Chunkapura in his interesting book, *The God of Rabindranath Tagore: A Study of the Evolution of His Understanding of God*,

> the reason for this apparent contradiction could be that the union with the Beloved that Tagore's heart sought was a permanent one, a union without the fear and the pain of separation, a meeting that knew no parting. Such a union was indeed 'not yet' and Tagore lives on in the hope of such a meeting with his Beloved, and feels that 'the long journey is still before him'... The living tension between the 'already' and the 'not yet', that is between what Rabindranath, the seeker, has already been able to realize and what yet remains beyond his reach ... [is because] 'spiritual longing is not just to find God, but to be united with him'.[25]

Though disappointed by Man and its modern civilization, Tagore remained a seeker of God and in search of Man's unity with Him. However, the great contribution of Tagore was not only to be an admirer of Nature and a seeker of God but also to have a lifelong commitment to the idea of unity of all reality. As such, by putting forward his concepts of Man and God, Tagore expanded his spiritual and poetic experiences to the frontiers of education and dialogue of cultures. Tagore knew well that without enlightenment and a genuine concept of education as a process which unfolds the dynamic character of life and society from the depths of Truth, Beauty, and Goodness, the unity of mankind would not be possible. He, therefore, advised contact with living Nature and meeting with life where it is supreme. We can see here the close link which exists between Tagore's vision of Nature and his vision of social awareness. That is to say, for Tagore, social awareness is the outcome of the inner being that fully endorses the welfare of each and every natural being. That is why Rabindranath suggests a shared experience of Truth as part of the Truth of God. And yet, he refuses to separate between plural experiences of Truth and the Truth of Man. He wrote:

> It is not impossible to imagine, nay it is easier to think, of one son in a Hindu family being Christian, another Moslem, and a third Vaisnava, but living together as one in the love of the parents. This is the real truth, and therefore, the good and the beautiful. The situation we are in today is not the truth. It is a hindrance to truth – I consider it the nightmare of our society … it is opposed to the 'religion of man'.[26]

Tagore was in search of the harmony of the whole in everyday life of human beings. It was the wholeness of the world and not antagonism among individuals, communities or cultures which was important to him. Tagore was in search of a synthesis between the old and the new, the east and the west. He, therefore, saw all cultures and all religions in their quest for the infinite. That is the reason why Rabindranath called for a real rapprochement of the souls between the east and the west, far from the number of things, but rather in their harmonious connectedness. Driven by the unity of life, Tagore writes in *Sadhana*:

> It fills me with great joy and a high hope for the future of humanity when I realize that there was a time in the remote past when our poet-prophets stood under the lavish sunshine of an Indian sky and greeted the world with the glad recognition of kindred. It was not

> an anthropomorphic hallucination. It was not seeing man reflected everywhere in grotesquely exaggerated images, and witnessing the human drama acted on a gigantic scale in nature's arena of flitting lights and shadows. On the contrary, it meant crossing the limiting barriers of the individual, to become more than man, to become one with the All. It was not a mere play of the imagination, but it was the liberation of consciousness from all the mystifications and exaggerations of the self. These ancient seers felt in the serene depth of their mind that the same energy, which vibrates and passes into the endless forms of the world, manifests itself in our inner being as consciousness; and there is no break in unity. For these seers there was no gap in their luminous vision of perfection. They never acknowledged even death itself as creating a chasm in the field of reality. They said, His reflection is death as well as immortality. They did not recognize any essential opposition between life and death, and they said with absolute assurance. 'It is life that is death.' They saluted with the same serenity of gladness 'life in its aspect of appearing and in its aspect of departure' – Then which is past is hidden in life, and that which is to come. They knew that mere appearance and disappearance are on the surface like waves on the sea, but life which is permanent knows no decay or diminution. Everything has sprung from immortal life and is vibrating with life, for life is immense.[27]

It is within such a philosophical framework that Tagore makes us conscious that we are in the process of rebirth of a new humanity. It is in this sense that Tagore is a true Renaissance man. His search for a life that, in his own words, is immense is primarily the struggle for the value of dialogue among cultures. To that end, Tagore remained a whole man, interested not only in poetry, philosophy and education but also open to other forms of living. And as he apprehended the nature of change in the world, he understood that there was no other way for cultures to have an exchange except through a new form of universal humanism. As it appears clearly, in all his thoughts and actions, Rabindranath Tagore brought a different dimension to the sense of belonging to a culture or a community by arguing for universal humanism. As a matter of fact, Tagore had the courage to defy and to break away from a narrow and fanatic concept of nationalism by considering the awakening of cultures as a historical moment in the process of the universalist awakening of the world. Consequently, from Tagore's point of view, matters of everyday life seemed of little consequence in the grand search for the organic wholeness and harmony of the universe. As a strong believer in the dignity of the individual and the value of universality, Tagore's vision of a new humanism finds its bedrock in the idea of the Whole Man as the Universal Mind. In other words, the history of mankind is the process of representation of the Universal in particular cultures. Tagore believes that mankind is united by a spiritual unity, of which different cultures and civilizations are distinctive notes in a musical symphony. Therefore, ultimately, material prosperity is but a means to attain the end of cultural fulfilment of Man, enabling it to gather all its experiences in the universal process of becoming a Universal Mind.

With such a vision impregnating his thoughts and actions, Tagore naturally felt that there was no other way to attain the Universal Mind than through a harmonious mutuality and a cosmic companionship between cultures. The centrality and the primacy of Tagore's Universal Man are even more explicitly stated in his efforts for the rapprochement of civilization and dialogue of cultures. In Tagore's own words: 'Man has come to the beginning of a world which has to be created by his own will and power … Man is now upon his career of creative life; he is to give from his abundance.'[28] This was a cry of hope out of the great heart of a 'Revered Master' (Gurudev) who was incapable of indifference to the fate of humanity. Almost a hundred years before Tagore's birth, the German philosopher of history, Johann Gottfried von Herder held that 'there are no immutable, universal, eternal rules or criteria of judgment in terms of which different cultures and nations can be graded in some single order of excellence … Every society, every age, has its own cultural horizons … Every age, every society, differs in its goals and habits and values from every other.'[29] In the same line of thought, Tagore wrote: 'It is high time for us to know how much more important it is, in the present age, to be able to understand the fundamental truths of all religions and realize their essential unity, thus clearing the way for a world-wide spiritual comradeship, than to preach some special religion of our own with all its historical limitations.'[30] At the very least, then, a study of Tagore's idea of dialogue of cultures will helps us to understand that culture is not a dead artifact, but a living entity and an active process that is in a constant state of regeneration.

2

Tagore and Dialogue of Cultures

'There is only one history – the history of man', wrote Tagore in his essay on *Nationalism*. By putting forward his concept of 'one history', he comes back to his idea of the shared fate of human civilizations. As a matter of fact, Tagore was not only an original philosopher of culture, well grounded in his own tradition and open to the western canon, but he was also one of the forerunners of intercultural dialogue in the twentieth century. Tagore, therefore, firmly believed in the principle of equal respect for all religious and cultural traditions of the world. His great insights into Indian civilization and its spiritual ethos did not prevent him from not appreciating the value of other civilizations. We can, therefore, say that Tagore understood the logic of cultural pluralism better than any other Indian in his time. For him, pluralism was not a spiritual concept but a philosophical attitude based on the rejection of cultural monism. Tagore's philosophical interpretation of human life was not established on the moral and ontological superiority of one culture over others. He believed that human beings were capable of understanding each other and having common values. In other words, he considered pluralism as an ontological self-expression of Man as a cultural being. That is why Tagore believed that cultures could interact and empower each other. He was also convinced that cultural coexistence goes hand in hand with a pluralist vision of peace and an intercultural alliance.

As an avid advocate of intercultural dialogue, Tagore was persuaded by the necessity of a symbiosis between the east and the west. He wrote:

> I have been fortunate in coming into close touch with individual men and women of the Western countries and have felt with them their sorrows and shared their aspirations. I have known that they seek the same God, who is my God – even those who deny Him. I feel certain that, if the great light of culture be extinct in Europe, our horizon in the East will mourn in darkness. It does not hurt my pride to acknowledge that, in the present age, Western humanity has received its mission to be the teacher of the world; that her science, through the mastery of laws of nature, is to liberate human souls from the dark dungeon of matter … The most significant fact of modern days is this, that the West has met the East. Such a momentous meeting of humanity, in order to be fruitful, must have in its heart some great emotional idea, generous and creative.[1]

Interestingly, despite his critique of western militarism and the absence on the European continent, Tagore was very much a believer in human solidarity in the context of a plurality of cultures. In a letter to Foss Westcott, Tagore argued: 'Believe me, nothing would give me greater happiness than to see the people of the West and the East march in a common crusade against all that robs the human spirit of its significance.'[2] Moreover, he replied to Kipling's remark that the east and the west were too divergent and 'never the twain shall meet' by affirming,

> Earnestly I ask the poet of the western world to realize and sing … with all the great power of music which he has, that the East and West are ever in search of each other, and that they must meet not merely in the fullness of physical strength, but in fullness of truth; that the right hand, which wields the sword, has the need of the left, which holds the shield of safety.[3]

As such, the ground reality for Tagore was that each one of us can cut across the boundaries of race, religion and nationality and engage in a dialogic understanding of diverse cultures.

Tagore's spiritual and intellectual call for diminishing the tension and the divide between nations was based on the very fact that he considered no culture to be a monolithic, rigid and static entity. In this regard,

> Tagore understood that an 'exclusive political culture' imposed upon people an unevenness that made some people, groups or an entire society more equal than others ... He, therefore, committed himself to spiritual-interculturality to collect together treasures of different cultures and to 'co-ordinate the study of all these different cultures – the Vedic, the Puranic, the Buddhist, the Jain, the Islamic, the Sikh and the Zoroastrian'... Tagore understood that claims to purity of cultures are untenable. He, therefore, perceived hospitality to cultures' diversity and/or culture-transmission, which would bring the harmony of active co-operation, as a crucial component of education and that was invariably intertwined with his realisation of spiritual-interculturality, the Upanisadic idea of the 'one-ness'. In other words, for Tagore, the realisation of spiritual-interculturality, the independence of the country and of education had become so intertwined as to be identical.[4]

Although convinced that moral progress lies in the direction of an intercultural alliance, Tagore insisted that cross-cultural learning was not something to be found as an accomplished phenomenon waiting to be recognized but as a permanent effort to rethink and recreate the idea of cultural pluralism. He believed that

> Man will have to make another great moral adjustment which will comprehend the whole world of men and not merely the fractional group of nationality. The call has come to every individual in the present age to prepare himself and his surroundings for this dawn

of a new era, when man shall discover his soul in the spiritual unity of all human beings.[5]

This concern for unity, which we can find in many of Tagore's essays, expresses his deep conviction that cross-cultural learning is a positive step in addressing the dangers that humanity faces in times of crisis. It is also, from his point of view, a sort of faith in the dialogical potential of human beings in building civilizational solidarities.

Tagore is a thinker who rejected sectarianism as 'a perverse form of worldliness in the disguise of religion'.[6] According to him, cultures could not survive unless they forged a plural space of interchange and discussion. That is why Tagore considered religious fundamentalism as a form of disease that created an obstruction to the friendship among cultures. He wrote in a letter to C. F. Andrews, dated 29 April 1921, 'It is a great good fortune to be accepted by one's fellow-beings from across the distance of geography, history and language, and through this fact we realize how truly One is the mind of Man, and what aberrations are the conflicts of hatred and the competitions of self-interest.'[7] Therefore, in Tagore's opinion, the universal culture should be based on the moral links among cultures and not on communitarian self-interests. 'To me', he said, 'the mere political necessity is unimportant, it is for the sake of our humanity, for the full growth of our soul, that we must turn our mind towards the ideal of the spiritual unity of man.'[8] Accordingly, for Tagore, a critique of cultural monism is a necessary condition for the realization of global harmony. However, he also takes his distance from all forms of cultural relativism because his system of thought is based on the idea that there is a common understanding of what it means to be a human being and how does this common humanity open us towards the otherness of the Other. Unlike some of his contemporaries, Tagore avoided the rather depressing conclusion that cultures are either superior or inferior to each other. From his point of view, one of the chief sources of misery in human history was to give priority to a given culture over the ideal of human solidarity. It is in this connection that he argued in *The Religion of Man* that 'the primitive barbarity of limitless suspicion and mutual jealousy fills the world's atmosphere today – the barbarity of the aggressive individualism of nations, pitiless in its greed, unashamed of its boastful brutality.'[9]

Throughout his life, Tagore uninterruptedly opposed uniformity and contrasted it to his ideal of unity of cultures. True unity, he asserted, was only possible in celebrating diversity through a dialogue among cultures. As such, the pursuit of harmony remained an ideal for Tagore beyond the imperatives of modern society and politics and a way for constantly analysing and understanding the changing world.

> Therefore, with a stoic resolve, he defended public liberties and insisted on the rights towards equality of all citizens regardless of race, class, caste, community, religion, language, colour, sex, and nation. Tagore did not distrust any culture because of its foreign character. He believed that the shock of outside forces was necessary for maintaining the vitality of India's traditional spiritual-intellectual culture and observed optimistically: 'European culture has come to us not only with its knowledge but also with its speed … [and] it is rousing our intellectual life from the inertia of formal habits. The contradiction it offers to our traditions makes our consciousness glow.'[10]

It is a fact that Tagore was not a politician, and he took his distance from politics. This is the feeling we get from his letter to William Rothenstein, written on 6 October 1920. He sums up his position in the following terms:

> I have nothing to do directly with politics. I am not a nationalist, moderate or immoderate in my political doctrine or inspiration. But politics is not a mere abstraction, it has its personality, and it does intrude into my life where I am human. It kills and maims individuals, it tells lies, it uses its sacred sword of justice for the

> purpose of massacre, it spreads misery broadcast over centuries of exploitation, and I cannot say to myself, 'Poet, you have nothing to do with these facts, for they belong to politics.'[11]

Reading this letter, one can surely get to the conclusion that Tagore is not presenting himself as a totally apolitical poet. Though not being on the side of party politics, Tagore, assuredly, took refuge in a certain mode of political thinking which guaranteed cultural pluralism. But he was fundamentally upset by the human tendency of dominating others. He was abhorred and disgusted by the communal violence in India that pushed people in their mental ghettos. In a letter to Leonard Elmhirst in 1939, he wrote the following: 'It does not need a defeatist to feel deeply anxious about the future of millions who … are being simultaneously subjected … the seething discontents of communalism.'[12]

Tagore's battle against communalism in India and beyond was certainly an effort to make not only his fellow countrymen but also citizens around the world realize the value of an intercultural imperative as a moral and intellectual quest in resisting prejudice and passiveness of the mind. But it's also interesting to see the extent to which Tagore's vision also leans towards the human heart. As he wrote, 'The heart of men is composed of rhythm, but due to the times, under the pressure of the machine, its rhythm is at present broken.'[13] Tagore's acquaintances and friendships during his trips to the east and the west intensified and consolidated his anti-communal thoughts and actions. As a result, his humanist sympathies were broadened, and he was totally convinced that the task of a cosmopolitan intellectual was to stand afar from its ivory tower. As an Indian writer who followed the Goethian concept of *Weltliteratur*, he saw himself at home and in the world. As Bidyut Chakrabarty affirms interestingly, 'Tagore's humanism was an outcome of the wisdom that he derived from multiple philosophical discourses. Besides the study of the Upanishads, Buddhism and western liberalism, the ideals that the Bengal Bauls propounded through their songs also acted as significant influences on his conceptual mould.'[14] We could certainly analyse these confluences of cultures in Tagore's life from a different philosophical angle. From the historical vantage point where Tagore stood as an 'educator of interculturality', he was influenced by a triple heritage. He was first and foremost influenced by the Upanishadic system of thought. Second, he was fully aware of the three monotheistic faiths, namely, Christianity, Islam and Judaism. Last, but not least, Tagore was also the Indian heir to the European humanist tradition. When Tagore argued for the universal value of culture, he was not arguing that people everywhere already acted according to this value, but rather that they had a good reason to see it as valuable. Tagore was not asking nations around the world to be deemed fit for universal culture; rather, he was asking all nations to become fit through universal culture. The force of Tagore's claim that universal culture plays an intrinsic importance in human life lies ultimately in the intercultural essence of the universal culture itself.

Tagore distanced himself from orthodox Hinduism. His favourite Hindu scriptures were the *Vedas* and the *Upanishads*. This is what he said about his contact with the Hindu scriptures: 'I was born to a family who were pioneers in the revival in our country of a religion based upon the utterance of Indian sages in the Upanishads … My father was the leader of a new religious movement, a strict monotheism, based upon the teachings of the Upanishads.'[15] Many commentators of Tagore have pointed to the deep and constructive influence of the *Upanishads* on Tagore's moral and religious philosophy. Ideas like 'Oneness', 'Supreme Person' and 'Unity in All', which we find in Tagore's essays, refer directly to the influence of the Hindu texts. As for the Christian influence on Tagore, we can hardly deny Tagore's sympathy for Jesus and his teaching, especially *The Sermon on the Mount*, but in a very similar way to Mahatma Gandhi, he had problems with the attitudes of some Christian missionaries. This negative attitude appears clearly in the following words of Tagore:

> Everyone knows that in the early stage of English education, a critical moment had arrived for our country … The whole society was agitated and the minds of the learned were perturbated. We had then started to feel ashamed of ourselves, thinking that in India, all the offering of poojas, all worships, was only the play of grown-up children; that there was never in this country, any high ideal of religion, or any true experience of God. Thus, the influence of the threat that the Christian missionaries had brought to our country at a time when the dignity of the Hindu society was being eroded, the minds of the educated were being torn apart, and the heart's lack of respect for one's own nation was making us weak, has still not totally faded from our hearts.[16]

Despite a few problems with the wrong interpretations of Christ's teachings, Tagore went along well with his lifelong Christian friends and collaborators, like C. F. Andrews and Leonard Elmhirst. Tagore had these kind words to say about Andrews: 'In no man have I seen such a triumph of Christianity.'[17] As for the civilizational influence of Christianity on Tagore, there is no doubt that the example of Christ and his teachings represented for him a strong example of the love of humanity. He wrote the following, only few months before his death in August 1941:

> Christianity has rendered love and respect to man … those who are really Christians have made known in every country, the love for man … We recognize that this religion knew how to unite mankind at least in one point, in the dedication to the neighbour. This is the highest recognition, for a religion. Wherever I saw excellence, be it in their literary works, be it in the behaviour of the people, there a marvellous humanity/humanness shines forth.[18]

Tagore was aware of the impact of modern Europe on India. However, he was also conscious about the limits of India's resistance against the west. While turning his back on western colonialism and imperialism, he accepted the contributions of Europe to science, philosophy and art. Once again, Tagore's primary concern was to unite the east and the west beyond all forms of prejudice and violence. He expressed his intercultural ethos in the following terms:

> We have to consider that the West is necessary to the East. We are complementary to each other because of our different outlooks upon life which have given us different aspects of truth. Therefore, if it be true that the spirit of the West has come upon our fields in the guise of a storm it is nevertheless scattering living seeds that are immortal. And when in India we become able to assimilate in our life what is permanent in Western civilization we shall be in the position to bring about a reconciliation of these two great worlds. Then will come to an end the one-sided dominance which is galling. What is more, we have to recognize that the history of India does not belong to one particular race but to a process of creation to which various races of the world contributed – the Dravidians and the Aryans, the ancient Greeks and the Persians, the Mohammedans of the West and those of central Asia. Now at last has come the turn of the English to become true to this history and bring to it the tribute of their life, and we neither have the right nor the power to exclude this people from the building of the destiny of India. Therefore, what I say about the Nation has more to do with the history of Man than specially with that of India.[19]

As such, for Tagore, the fundamental unity of civilizations was based on an inner rhythm, which he believed was broken both in the east and the west. Fully preoccupied by his mission of bringing east and west together, Tagore tried to establish a dialogue between different civilizations of Asia and the Middle East and the west. He knew the real value of universal culture. He was convinced that a creative force was needed

> to bring to realization the fundamental unity of the tendencies of different civilizations of Asia, thereby enabling the East to gain a

> full consciousness of its own spiritual purpose, the obscuration of which has been the chief obstacle in the way of true co-operation of East and West, the great achievements of those mutually complementary civilizations are alike necessary for Universal Culture in its completeness.[20]

The question remains: what had Tagore found in the [the?] western canon which was worthy of admiration? Tagore clarified his position in his Convocation Address at the University of Calcutta in 1937. He argued: 'Europe has provided the world with the gifts of a great culture – had it not the power to do so, it would never have attained its supremacy. It has given the example of dauntless courage, ungrudging self-sacrifice, it has shown tireless energy in the acquisition and spread of knowledge, in the making of institutions for human welfare.'[21] Tagore is, of course, thinking here of European civilization not in terms of the rise of nationalism and the First World War but in relation with the period of the Enlightenment, which had refined and reinforced India's intellectual circles in the mid-nineteenth century. However, the First World War turned Tagore's mind towards the violent features of the European civilization and against the idea of pluralism and interculturality, which he had supported all his life. While he continued to believe in Man and Unity, Tagore declared the decline of the core humanist values in Europe. He declared,

> During my boyhood days, the attitude of the cultured and educated section of Bengal, nurtured on English leaning, was charged with a feeling of revolt against rigid regulations of society … Then came … a painful feeling of disillusion when I began increasingly to discover how easily those who accepted the highest truths of civilization disowned them with impunity whenever questions of national self-interest was involved … I had at one time believed that the spring of civilization would issue out of the heart of Europe. But today when I am about to quit the world that faith has gone bankrupt altogether.[22]

Despite his dark despair, Tagore continued to have some hope for the victory of human solidarity and intercultural dialogue. Tagore strongly held an opinion that without education there is no future for humanity and nationalism, and sectarianism, communalism and religious fundamentalism will win. His moral and religious philosophy was moving towards the primacy of education in the process of safeguarding humanist universalism. In his doubts about the unethical character of universal civilization, Tagore came up with a negative image of science and scientists who are in the service of evil.

> In his *Raktakarabi* [*Red Oleanders*], a play that he rewrote ten times between 1923 and 1926, the King at the centre is actually a Man of Science, cooped up in his laboratory, who thinks himself the King, and is allowed to think so by his administrators / bureaucrats – the Sardars, the Mondais, the priest and the professor – who maintain a tyrannical authority devoted to accumulating wealth. The country is significantly named Yakshapuri. The *yaksha*, in Bengali popular mythology, guards and protects wealth in the nether world, deep below the surface of the earth. The dark holes of the mines are repositories of gold in Tagore's play, and the site of brutal exploitation and the stirrings of rebellion. The King, blind in his sense of the power that comes with knowledge, serves the interests of the makers of wealth, till his blinkers come off at the end of the play and he realizes that he has been 'deceived', thanks to the illumination that is brought to him by Nandini.[23]

We should not forget that Tagore's rage against war in Europe took new dimensions with the rise of fascism, civil war in Spain and the start of the Second World War. Eight months after Guernica was bombed by the Germans in 1937, Tagore wrote a demoralizing poem on the arrogant character of human civilization:

> The day my consciousness was released from the cave of dissolution,
> It drew me to the edge of a volcano spouting the flames of hell,
> All in a tumult of wonderment, spelling terrible calamity;

Its burning smoke roaring deep disdain of humanity,
Its ominous breathing shaking the earth;
Staining the air with a hue of black.
I saw the self-destructive idiotic frenzy of our time,
with the filthy mockery of corruption all over its body.
On one hand arrogant inhumanity,
The shameless vaunt of madness,
On the other the faltering footsteps of cowardice,
Clasping to its chest the treasured holdings of a miser,
With the moment's growl of a scared animal
Giving way to safe and silent acquiescence.
All the masters of States with mature authority
Hold back within their tight lips all orders arid decisions
In doubts and fears, while the monstrous birds
Rush into the troubled skies flight after flight,
From the banks of the river of death,
Vultures craving for human flesh, their mechanical wings in loud clamour,
Desecrating the sky. O Judge, seated on the throne of Eternal Time,
Give me strength, Bring the voice of thunder to my throat,
So that I can condemn this havoc that kills women and children,
A condemnation that will ring for ever in the very breathing of a shameful memory,
Even when this stifled, terrorized, shackled age,
Will be lost in silence in the ashes of its funeral pyre.[24]

Tagore was a pluralist and a believer in an intercultural world, where cultures learn freely and openly from each other. On the whole, we can say that Tagore was a thinker who had faith in the unifying tendency of human beings and the possibility of overcoming divisions, disunity and discord. According to Tagore, Man had a 'Spirit of Life' which provided humanity with a creative unity and helped the growth of culture and civilization. Having thus postulated the idea of organic unity of cultures and civilizations, Tagore points out in his book *The Religion of Man* to the central role of prophet-educators, who represent, according to him, 'the messengers of Man to men'. He explains:

> It is significant that all great religions have their historic origins in persons who represented in their life a truth which was not cosmic and unmoral, but human and good. They came as the messengers of Man to men of all countries and spoke of the salvation that could only be reached by the perfecting of our relationship with Man the Eternal, Man the Divine. Whatever might be their doctrines of God, or some dogmas that they borrowed from their own time and tradition, their life and teaching had the deeper implication of a Being who is the infinite in Man, the Father, the Friend, the Lover whose service must be realized through serving all mankind.[25]

Tagore considered educators, like prophets, as enlighteners of humanity. This is why his theory of universalism applies predominantly to education. 'Education', according to him,

> has for its object freedom-freedom of intellect, freedom of sympathy, freedom in the material universe through our truthful dealings with her universal laws, freedom in the society through our maintaining of truth and love in all human relationships. It is a most difficult ideal and that immense difficulty only proves the majesty of the human soul and the magnificence of our true civilisation.[26]

If we agree that Tagore's philosophy was one all-embracing vision of Man, God, Nature and Art, we can say that education played a central role in holding Man's life, mind and soul together. Despite its deniers, Tagore did have a strong and influential philosophy of education.

Having emphasized the attainment of unity through freedom of the individual and creative work, Tagore was fully conscious of the fact that education is a method of integration within a world wider than one's own. He, to sum up, tried to base his philosophy of education on the foundation of his moral and spiritual thoughts. He was fully aware of the difficulties and shortcomings of his educational task, but he believed that pedagogy was the only domain which could help to restore ethics in politics and prepare a future generation of peacemakers and cultural animators beyond religious and communal wars and clashes of civilizations. He poured out his heart of a poet and his experience of a sage of a unity spirit by writing the following in his essay 'A Poet's School' (1926):

> The minds of the children today are almost deliberately made incapable of understanding other people with different languages and customs. The result is that, later, they hurt one another out of ignorance and suffer from the worst form of the blindness of the age ... I have tried to save our children from such aberrations, and here the help of friends from the West, with their sympathetic hearts, has been of the greatest service.[27]

Let us not forget that Tagore's educational awareness for inclusive education and intercultural dialogue is the only way for us to understand and rediscover his philosophical wisdom. In that sense, Tagore is more than a common icon; he is an animator of new ideas, which, though not fully followed by Indians and other nations, will be part of our readings for the future.

3

Tagore's Educational Ideas

Tagore's greatest relevance lies in his philosophy of education. According to Kathleen M. O'Connell, one of the great specialists of Tagore's educational ideas,

> Looking at Tagore's 1929 educational concerns from a contemporary perspective, one feels that they continue to have great relevance, and that, were he living today, he would concentrate on many of the same aspects of education, though with even greater urgency. In education, one feels he would still be speaking 'in praise of leisure' and urging us to reclaim the quest for developing forms of education for our children and ourselves that allow for the full and joyous development of the creative personality.[1]

In tracing the significance and purpose of education in our world, Tagore insisted on the freedom of mind, the effervescence of imagination and empathy for the Other. He wrote in his essay, 'A Poet's School',

> I tried to create an atmosphere in my school – this was the main task. In educational institutions our faculties have to be nourished in order to give our mind its freedom, to make our imagination fit for the world which belongs to art, and to stir our sympathy for human relationships. This last is even more important than learning the geography of foreign lands.[2]

Undoubtedly, Tagore is among those educators, like Rousseau, Tolstoy and Thoreau, who did not believe in learning through the medium of books. This was a criticism that he addressed to all those who were against creative thinking in the matter of education, including the religious sectarians. He argued:

> The Christian missionaries themselves help in this cultivation of contempt for alien races and civilizations. In the name of brotherhood and in the blindness of sectarian pride they crate misunderstanding. These they make permanent in their textbooks and thereby poison the susceptible minds of the young. I have tried to save our children from such a mutilation of natural human love with the help of friends from the West who, with their sympathetic understanding, have done us the greatest service.[3]

As we can see, Tagore extended his criticism of religious sectarianism beyond Hinduism and to Christianity. Deeply sad and disappointed by the eruption of the First World War in the west, he started travelling to the United States and Japan in 1916–17, where he gave public lectures against nationalism. While condemning the dangers of nationalism, Tagore 'began laying the groundwork for an international educational centre that would facilitate communication between east and west, between races and cultures and different social strata. His learning centre was to be a place in harmony with nature, where the minds of the students would not be'[4] under the influence of indecent lies of nationalist ideologies.

Tagore was against the idea of brainwashing children's minds through education. He believed that the continuous growth of the mind of the child should take place in a natural environment. According to him, education lost its value when 'divorced from the streams of life and confined within the four walls of the classroom.'[5] Sympathy and human solidarity are the two essential aspects of Tagore's theory of education. Here, we find, once again, his ideal of human solidarity and his insistence on the multifaceted and plural essence of humanity. To foster this sense of plurality in mankind constitutes the basic aim of Tagore's philosophy of education. The aim of education should be the growth and the meeting of minds.

According to Tagore, only 'a meeting of minds makes a university true'.[6] Hence, he believed that a community which tries itself as a plural entity needs to learn and understand the others for its own mental nourishment and spiritual growth. Thus, Tagore considered pluralist education as an innovative action in the public sphere. For him, culture is not a dead artefact but a living process which is in constant regeneration. Therefore, Tagore believed that if a community's culture is to remain alive, its members need to continually reinterpret their traditions according to their own time and circumstances. Still more crucial, for Tagore, was the idea that plurality could not function in strict adherence to existing cultural practices. As such, the existence of plurality presupposed a life committed to the reinterpretation and adaptation of current practices. It was Tagore's opinion that pluralism could be found, at least in embryos, in many cultures, including those whose dominant values were 'non-western'. Not surprisingly, Tagore's programme of self-empowerment through education became the essential principle of what human solidarity and a plural world could offer humanity. In other words, Tagore's faith in human capacity of listening and learning helped him to engage with other cultures and to reach across their differences to find a common ground for cooperation.

We should admit that no one in modern Indian culture has thought as radically as Rabindranath Tagore on the need to accomplish a mediation between the particular and the universal, just as no one as Tagore has produced such a startlingly ambitious attempt to think pluralism in terms of a pedagogy of empathy. To Tagore, education promotes the ethos of fairness and social justice. As Tagore affirms,

> today there is a variety of subjects for education. It is no longer possible to cover a diversity of instructions through old mythological tales alone. Yet if our aim is to eliminate the distinction between the educated and the uneducated classes then those who have been deprived must learn about many things to which they had

> no access … If we think more about it we find that the difference in the level of knowledge between the two classes is most apparent in their knowledge of history. They are unable to join the efforts of the educated classes because they cannot fathom the thoughts and ideas of the former, because the common people are unaware of how at home and abroad people have elevated themselves, gathered strength, formed parties, wrested what they thought was their due and having got them consolidated their gains. It is the depth of ignorance not to know what men have achieved in the world and what they are capable of achieving.[7]

It is clear that Tagore's educational thoughts originate from his social philosophy. Tagore was the first Indian educationist to observe a close link between social criticism and the *raison d'etre* of education. His criticism of the Indian system of education covered both the ancient and the modern. In a famous piece written in 1913, he argued:

> Social changes are always taking place and will continue to do so. No one can stop it. Nothing can be more calamitous for people than to freeze all systems permanently in a traditional mode. This is somewhat like the odd situation where the river is changing course but the jetty for the ferryboats remains in one fixed place. To go any other place is to be socially ostracised. So, we have a situation where there is a jetty but there is no water and there are boats for ferrying, but they cannot ply. In such circumstances, the society is not allowing us the education which is suited to the times. It is imparting an education which was relevant two or three thousand years ago. Therefore, the biggest school of learning to be a human being is closed to us. It has no claims on our current lifestyle … Today's Brahman is unable to impart an education acquired through severe self-discipline, but he is free with the dust of his feet for the inferior castes to touch … The bird and the chain must remain intact, although the bird is long dead … Therefore when the society has not kept open any way to have a healthy harmony with

> the flow of its own lifestyle and consequently the obsolete system proves a hurdle at every step, stifling it, then, it not only denies us the most natural and easy school of learning, but worst of all it does not allow truth to prevail and only accumulates falsehoods.[8]

In arguing in this fashion, Tagore was quite clear and transparent about his position on what he considers as the end of the Brahmanical education in India. However, he also did not hide his opinion concerning teachers and schoolmasters who followed the so-called 'national' schooling system. Tagore makes an important point here in terms of living in truth in matters of education:

> We were taught a great truth about education, namely that man can learn from another human being, just as a water-tank is filled only with water, a flame is lit by another, and life alone can infuse life. If you truncate a man, he is no longer a human being but a material for the office, the court or the mills; instead of being human he wants to be a schoolmaster. He is then unable to inspire life; he can only give lessons from textbooks. Education can flow like bloodstream in the body, only when the relationship the teacher and the pupil is full and intimate … We cannot buy or accept only in parts, the best things in life, affection, and love alone can help us absorb them … There is nothing more terrible in childhood than a lifeless teaching, because it crushes out more than it gives to the mind. We seek for our social system the teacher who can impart movement in our life and for our educational system we are looking for the teacher who will free our minds from all obstacles.[9]

If one considers these issues put forward herewith by Tagore, one may arrive at the conclusion that he was deeply disappointed by the state of education at the national level. Yet, Tagore was searching for an educational institution which could transcend all national centres for education and which could stand as a universal centre for human studies. Tagore started his own school at Santiniketan in 1901, away from his family house in Calcutta. In the beginning, there were only five students, but by 1913 Santiniketan became a well-known school and Tagore's own personality was at the centre of interest of many visitors like William Rothenstein, Anand Coomaraswamy and Mahatma Gandhi. Thus, by 1917, Santiniketan started attracting students from all over India, and in December 1918 Visva-Bharati Bhavan was born, which by 1921 was replaced by Visva-Bharati University.

With Visva-Bharati in the global picture, Tagore was considered no more only as the greatest of India and the first Asian writer to win the Nobel Prize in Literature but also the founder and the first Vice Chancellor of Visva-Bharati University. According to Sabyasachi Bhattacharya,

> the central idea was captured very well in the words Tagore made the motto of the university: *Yatra visva bhavati ekanidam*, i.e., this is where the entire world meets in a single nest … Modern education, particularly science and a scientific world-outlook, Tagore said, must be naturalized in the Indian soil and the opportunity for education must not be limited to the top of society leaving untouched layers below. Tagore made a concrete suggestion which anticipated the idea of Open University – a syllabus to be announced, and examination to be conducted by the University of Calcutta without requiring school or college attendance and payment of fees. The plan, needless to say, was rejected by the University authorities of the day.[10]

We need to return to the Tagorean concept of 'unity', which is at the heart of his philosophy of education. Tagore looked upon his concept of education as an organic idea that grows around understanding and respect of unity. Incidentally, Tagore approached the concept of unity in a non-political context. In an article on cooperative education, published in September 1920, he affirmed:

> We need in our country, a large field for collaboration in education where there will be constant exchange and evaluation of learning, where Indian scholarship has to be judged against the backdrop

> of the evolution of the learning of the world as a whole … Those who look at only one aspect of India distinct from the integrated whole also have not realized the true Indian psyche within their own minds. This is the reason why we have developed no respect for the unity which is deeper and greater than mere political unity. That which is universal and eternal foundation of all unities in this world is true unity. It is unity of minds, a unity of souls. India has to recognise the unity of minds as greater than political unity. Because then alone can India invite the world at large to its own abode.[11]

Once again, we find here some of the key elements of Tagore's philosophy: unity of mind is required for allowing the attainment of universality and development of empathy among the students; true knowledge can flourish only in the absence of sectarianism and nationalistic approaches to education; and finally, free generation and transmission of knowledge can bring about creative minds.

Tagore tried hardly to apply his educational ideas and pedagogical approaches to the world around him, but his pessimism about the future of Santiniketan and Visva-Bharati appeared clearly in his letters to his friends and his appeal to Mahatma Gandhi in 1935 to accept these institutions under his protection. Perhaps towards the end of his life and despite the companionship of individuals like Gandhi, Tagore felt very lonely and worried about the future of Visva-Bharati. Once again, what occupied his mind was his own loneliness and the indifference of the world towards all the evils which separated human beings. In a meaningful essay titled 'Co-operation', Tagore explored profoundly the consequences of the absence of fellowship. He argued:

> Man loses his true stature when he fails to unite fully with his fellows. A complete man is one who has this capacity for union, a lone individual is a fragmented being … At one time the co-operative principle was followed to some extent in our village-based economy. But life now is not as simple as in those days. But life was not as simple in those days. Besides it is now far more

> difficult for the rich to be selfless. The masses must now develop their own inherent strength that will be more permanent worth. If the Indian economy is based once more on co-operation, the villages which are the nurseries of our civilization will be vitalized and the whole country will gain a new life.[12]

It goes without saying that for Tagore, the essential condition for the existence of education is plurality. According to him, the very basic Truth is that individuals live with others and alone by themselves. So, people come together to establish a common ground and to take the initiative and create an institution. This space of shared values is thus the basic condition of plurality and togetherness of human beings. For Tagore, the creation of an educational institution like Visva-Bharati testified to the ability of Indians and others to foster the conditions of plurality. However, what Tagore emphasizes time and again is that human beings must be careful not to get attuned to the mechanistic world where greed replaces empathetic interconnectedness.

> The more the greed the less is the compunction to do others down. But greed is not a philosophy, it is a deadly sin. It has no mission to create. Therefore, when it occupies the central place in any civilization then the spiritual link between people begins to snap in that civilization. To the extent it gathers wealth and power and widens opportunities to do so, the spiritual identity of man is weakened to that extent.[13]

Tagore considered education as a form of self-creation and self-realization. That is why Tagore calls on us to recognize that in an educating process the task of the individual is as important as that of the society. It is with this in mind that he argues against the danger to short-circuit education of children and youngsters by asserting sectarian and fanatical truths. Therefore, as a process of companionship and mutual understanding, education does not represent an absolute Truth and a means by which to arrive at power.

Moreover, every claim in the sphere of education to an absolute Truth strikes at the very roots of character-building and human formation. In his incessant interventions, Tagore pointed out the fact that the world we share in common can be seen through many windows, some opaque and others more transparent. As we can see, like much of the tradition of American pragmatists, especially John Dewey, Tagore had a strong commitment to an intersubjective and non-instrumentalist view of education. According to Francis Assisi Samuel,

> Dewey and Tagore opposed the theory of dualism. They did not perceive reality in dualities; rather, they saw the dialectics of reality … Dewey addressed the problem of dualism through his theory of nature, experience, continuity, and interaction. Tagore solved the problem through his theory of harmony and fullness … Dewey and Tagore, thus, did not perceive the individual and society in opposition as in the traditional philosophy or as in the liberal individualism of modern times. They viewed them rather in an organic relationship and complementary to each other … [As such], the individual, for Dewey and Tagore, was unique, free, inviolable, and moral. On account of their profound respect for the dignity of the human person, they condemned the abuse of the individual, whether it be slavery, the caste system, or similar discrimination based on cultural or economic status.[14]

For Tagore, the interaction between the society and the individual took place through education. Education, as a practice of listening, learning and being close to Nature, would free the individual's mind from the tyranny of the material world. Tagore's reverence for human dignity and the nobility of spirit conflicted with the reality of a meaningless individual in a meaningless world. Thus, he looked upon his idea of education as an ontological communion between the individual and the world. Tagore went on to argue that the search for

Truth should replace the quest for greed. He wrote in an essay entitled 'The Unity of Education':

> Why should greed be condemned? Because it does not lead to truth – so the *Isa Upanishad* answers. And to people who say that they do not care for truth, but only for enjoyment, the Upanishad answers, 'Enjoy by all means. But then, there is no joy without truth' … Truth confers unity, while wealth brings about disunity … One aspect of spiritual culture concerns the freeing of the soul from the oppression off the material universe. This is in the groundwork of culture, and it is today in the charge of the West … Unity of East and West will achieve the unity of spiritual and scientific knowledge. Because they are not united, the East is poverty – haunted and lifeless, and the West without peace and unhappy.[15]

For the old Tagore, the sage of Visva-Bharati, India's immediate problems were not political but spiritual and pedagogical. He believed that the whole world needed a spiritual process of learning to liberate its mind. Tagore also questioned the cultural and social imperatives which required the Indians to choose the caste system. Therefore, for him, finding solutions to the caste system and poverty were much more urgent than some political decisions taken by the Indian Congress Party. Tagore's

> hope was that if India could establish equanimity between the various races and religious groups through a basis of social co-operation and regeneration of the spirit, then she could hold herself as a model of unity for the rest of the world … Tagore was of the view that such unity and plurality of consciousness could be achieved only through proper education of the people, eradication of poverty through modernisation and cultivation of freedom of thought and imagination.[16]

While fully aware of the distance that separated him from the Indian political opinion during the independence movement, Tagore had the courage to confront his critics, including Mahatma

Gandhi, and defended his vision of pluralism against all types of regimentation and exclusion. In the same manner, Tagore abhorred the social and economic inequalities in Indian society and considered the caste system as a shame and disgrace for Indian society. Taking all these circumstances into account, we can argue that Tagore continues to be, until this day, the great outsider to twentieth-century Indian intellectual thought. His philosophical essays were disturbingly unorthodox and strikingly dissenting. This was partly due to the fact that Tagore made great efforts to communicate his ideas. Also, for him, writing was part of the process of changing the world. However, this did not mean that others always shared his views and were not prisoners of misreading his books. On the contrary, Tagore suffered enormously from the number of ways in which his thoughts gave rise to misunderstandings. In a letter to C. F. Andrews, written from New York, he explained: 'I am afraid I shall be rejected by my own people when I go back to India. My solitary cell is awaiting me in my motherland. In their present state of mind, my countrymen will have no patience with me, who believes God to be higher than my country.'[17]

The anti-systematic mode of thinking, to which Tagore was profoundly committed, was something which kept his thought nonconformist and non-complacent. It was in this spirit that he developed his ideas of unity, wholeness, harmony and fellowship around his multiple experiences of plurality. This is important because what keeps Tagore's work relevant is that many of the things that he had to say look quite important, not to say urgent, for today's world. As a matter of fact, many of our concerns, including the environmental crisis and the decline of education and critical thinking in our world, invite us to look more often on the side of Tagore as a sage and an educator. The overwhelming message of his 'Crisis in Civilization' in 1941 could be read today as a humanist appeal to global responsibility. The ethical message with which Tagore said his adieu to the world was a humanist message of despair and hope together. He wrote: 'Perhaps the new dawn will come from this horizon, from the East where the sun rises; and then, unvanquished man will retrace his path of conquest, despite all barriers, to win back his lost heritage.'[18] No doubt, Tagore's pessimistic thoughts grew directly out of his experiences and commitments in different fields of education, ethics and aesthetics. Meanwhile, his investigation of how civilizations could have turned into forms of fanaticism and nationalistic ideologies led him to look beyond his desperation and unhappiness and find the remote reasons for the emergence of these inhuman forces within the cultural acceptance of monistic visions in different communities. Therefore, instead of drawing the usual battle line between modernity and tradition, Tagore drew the line between the universal human spirit and national narcissism and chauvinism. From Tagore's point of view the nationalistic ideologies of the twentieth century had/have the power of turning human beings into meaningless animals. The crucial point is that in Tagore's account, masses of nationalistic ideologies believe that everything is possible and that the world can become the product of their diabolical imagination.

At the heart of Tagore's understanding of the decline of empathic humanism lies a drive towards unlimited control over Nature and human beings. According to Tagore, one of the side effects of the crisis in civilization is the divergence between the villages and the towns. He develops this idea in an essay written in 1928 entitled 'City and Village'. He writes the following:

> The task before us today is to make whole the broken-up communal life, to harmonize the divergence between village and town, between the classes and the masses, between the pride of power and the spirit of comradeship. Those who rely on revolution to achieve this end seek to curtail truth in order to make it easy. When they are after enjoyment, they shun renunciation; when they incline to renunciation, they would banish enjoyment from the land and

> subdue man's mind by cramping it. What we, of Visva-Bharati, say, is that the nature of man is denied if truth is not offered to him in its wholeness. From this deprivation comes his despair and his ailments ... Civilization has grown by the conjunction of man's intellect with the gifts of Nature. These two must always work in partnership. Whenever the acquisitions of the intellect are hoarded in some strong room, the store goes on dwindling. We cannot live long on the accumulations of a bygone age.[19]

Truly speaking, creating a modern nation state is not among the Tagorean ideals. For the good reason that Tagore sees politics as the expression of the personality of a civilization and a people. With Tagore, the poet and the philosopher, the stress of the argument is on the concept of 'respect'. Tagore invites us to respect one another, to respect Nature and the world and to respect life and Truth. He underlines:

> The shastras say: *Shraddyaya] deyam* – if you give, then give with respect. That is how I set to work ... If we could free even one village from the shackles of helplessness and ignorance, an ideal for the whole of India would be established. That is what occurred to me then and that is what I still think. Let a few villages be rebuilt in this way, and I shall say they are my India. That is the way to discover the true India.[20]

Tagore, like Gandhi, believed that the true India is the India of villages, not cities. However, all his life he blamed himself for being a 'zamindar'. Being an inheritor of the system of landlordism in colonial Bengal was a difficult task for Tagore and made him ashamed. In a letter to his son Rathindra on 31 October 1930 he wrote:

> In the era that is upon us, we can no longer depend on our zamindari for income. My mind has been rebelling against it from way back and the feeling is now definite ... the whole business of zamindari makes me ashamed ... I feel sad to think that from childhood we have been raised parasites ... At certain historical

> conjunctures everyone must suffer; indeed, everyone is already experiencing this; it is wrong to expect to remain comfortable by evading the crisis.[21]

What we can understand from Tagore's letter is that his worries are more ethical by nature and less financial. Though he was deeply concerned by the survival of Visva-Bharati due to the Great Depression of 1934 affecting his estates, Tagore also reacted vividly to the act of going around and begging for financial aid. In arguing in this fashion, Tagore showed the true, noble nature of his spirit. After all, his ultimate aim in education, philosophy or literature was to claim the universality which resides in the heart and the mind of mankind forever. For Tagore, the symphony created by literature belonged to the humanity of all times, expressed by the concept of the Universal Man. He said:

> Only when we realize that Literature reveals the universal man (*visva-manab*), we shall see what is the essence of literature … Consider how man has extended his self in the tangible world into an intangible self … Confined as he is in his location in the outer world, in his intangible creations he enlarges his self, and this second universe is his own creation, that is what literature is about.[22]

After following Tagore's thought train, we must concede that in the course of his responses to the problems of his time, Tagore also made the world conscious by one word: the word 'nationalism'. As a matter of fact, the unnatural growth of nationalism in the first half of the twentieth century provided Tagore with the indispensable framework within which he developed his own original political philosophy. It is not surprising that this aspect of Tagore's thought has been largely studied. The period of catastrophic change and international chaos out of which it arose was followed by the Second World War, that Tagore did not live long to see the end. Nevertheless, his last writings show the level of his cultural pessimism and political distress. However, the interesting point here is that although Tagore's political and philosophical thoughts did indeed arise out of specific events happening in India and around the world, they went on to trace fascinating reflections and meditations in the realm of ideas. Tagore's questions on the decline of civilization and the rise of barbarism are still ours. Can we find lasting ideas and institutions which can rescue us from the darkness of the great perils of history? The development and outcome of Tagore's reflections on this final question will occupy us next.

4

The Crisis in Civilization and Nationalism

Rabindranath Tagore was a poet–philosopher who was not indifferent to the shaping forces of his age. As a multilingual intellectual, he was quite at ease with the idea of travelling and learning from other cultures. As Ana Jelnikar points out accurately,

> 'Seeing and recognizing reality also in human beings outside his immediate environment, and beyond instrumentality of power, allowed Tagore to experience closeness across cultural divides, and this closeness, he found, was largely reciprocated. It was indeed possible to come into touch with, in his words, "the Eternal Man amongst unknown humanity in a foreign country."'[1]

Tagore was among those Indian intellectuals who understood that the globalization of modernity was an irreversible fact, which had to be sought through intercultural dialogues. He affirmed:

> The spirit of the modern age has cast its radiance from the western horizon, illumining the entire span of world history. The mind of Europe, under some tremendous urge, has projected itself into every corner of the earth … Here in India we are still conditioned by our surrender to the fatalism of the almanac, but there are gaps in our walls through which the European spirit has forced itself to our inner yard. It has brought us the great gift of knowledge in its universal aspects. It has wakened us to the all-pervasive inquiry of the intellect, keenly seeking to probe into the innermost nature of whatever is near at hand or far away, whether big or small, whether of practical or of theoretical value. It has demonstrated that knowledge is indivisible and one unbreakable thread runs through all phenomena.[2]

By reading these words, we can draw the conclusion that for Tagore the time was ripe to step outside the unchanging and unvarying view of civilizations and to prepare the true foundations of reconciliation and harmony among cultures.

Tagore believed in the meeting of minds across various cultures and different traditions of thought. His personal journey took him from east to west and back to India. As it was discussed in previous chapters, Tagore had an evolutionary view of humanity, drawing on both the enlightening teachings of Rammohun Roy and his own experiences of nationalist India. Tagore's own presence in the culture of early-twentieth-century India was partly due to the influence of his father, Debendranath, as one of the spiritual leaders of the *Brahmo Samaj* in nineteenth-century Bengal. However, we should not minimize the original trajectory of Tagore himself and his role in the context of the Indian intellectual awareness. As Michael Collins suggests,

> We can certainly take note of the basic fact that Rabindranath's grandfather was a co-founder of the Brahmo movement with Rammohun Roy, that his father revitalised the movement and that his brothers were active and dedicated members of the Adi Brahmo Samaj. This suggest that, in general terms, Rabindranath's life and thought had to have been affected at a general level by a particular set of historical circumstances. But at the level of the particular, Tagore himself was keen to stress the individual nature of his thinking, and there are reasonably objective grounds from which to support the idea of a strong sense of agency and intentionality on Tagore's part.[3]

It is crucial to understand that Tagore's creative force, that was related to his conception of political freedom, found its strongest manifestation in his 'vision of national integration which he called the ocean of humanity'.[4] Looking back upon Tagore's life and work, it becomes very clear that his acceptance of other cultures, including the west, was a result of a fundamental unity of spirit that Tagore wished to stress as a task of 'building up of great India'. As such, Tagore's early essays on the east–west encounter were deeply focused on a particular dialogical approach from the angle of India's civilizational self-discovery and cultural maturity. This is very clear in an essay entitled 'The Future of India', published by Tagore in 1911. He declared: 'If we turn our face aside, if we isolate ourselves, if we refuse to accept any new element, we shall still fail to resist the march of time, we shall fail to impoverish and defraud Indian history. The highest intellects of our country in the modern age have spent their lives at the task of reconciling the West to the East.'[5]

Tagore's intentions seemed very clear: as a colonized Indian, he sought to establish a bridge with western modernity without necessarily demonizing the west. His attack against Indian anti-colonial nationalism was also a way to recover India's soul, open to modern knowledge and service to humanity, without getting involved in religious or nationalist ideological divides between spirituality and nation. As he wrote to Andrews,

> I, personally do not believe that Europe is wholly and entirely materialistic. She has lost her faith in religion but not in humanity. Man in his essential nature can never be solely materialistic. In Europe the ideals of human activity are truly spiritual; for these ideals are not paralysed by shackles of scriptural injunctions, or, to put it another way, their sanction lies in the heart of man and not in something external to him. This freedom from changeless, irrational bondage or external regulations, is a very big asset of modern European civilisation. In Europe man is pouring forth his life for knowledge, for the land of his birth and in the service of humanity, through the urge of his own innate ideals and not because some revered pundit has ordained it, nor because the scriptures or regulations of orthodoxy have indicated such action. It is this attitude of mind which is essentially spiritual.[6]

Tagore's position in this letter goes directly against Gandhi's *Hind Swaraj*, where the future Mahatma (as named by Tagore) pointed to the tension between India and the west in terms of a conflict between materialism and spiritual values. However, though Tagore and Gandhi did not agree on the importance of the emerging global modernity to humanity, they both believed that India's unique contribution to the modern world should be more spiritual than anything else. As an Aufklärer (enlightener), Tagore certainly prized the maturity of the human mind more than anything else. His quest for an empathetic humanism was assuredly a big part of his process of the 'building up' of India. As such, in terms of human history, Tagore saw India's contribution to humanity, and against fanaticism and extremism, as what he called a 'middle point'. He wrote:

> Man is being called from two sides by self and others, acquisition and giving away, self-restraint and freedom, custom and reason; the true education of humanity consists in learning how to balance both forces, so as to reach the middle point. Human history is the history of efforts to acquire this balancing power. India affords us the means of clearly observing the picture of the quest of this harmony.[7]

Tagore was very conscious of his difficult intellectual position in early-twentieth-century India as a middle point. He, therefore, tried to balance his high expectations regarding India with the radicalized political situation on the ground. While being critical about the imperial face of English politics, he continued criticizing his fellow Indians for their chauvinism and cruelty. He argued:

> I shall not lose faith in humanity or lack the assurance that in English politics morality is even greater truth than power; although I am daily confronted with evidence to the contrary, and find the English given to selfishness, love of power, greed, anger, cowardice, and pride. These faults of the English hurt us only because we have them ourselves, because we too are easily frightened and easily

> tempted, and bear in our hearts envy, malice, and distrust. But if we are great and heroic; generous, virtuous and trustful; and if we possess the greatness which our enemy possesses, we shall then win, morally if not physically and in spite of the injuries caused by our enemy's faults. It is our own cowardice that makes us underestimate the merits of the British Government and overestimate its faults.[8]

In the same line of thought, Tagore reacted to the Amritsar massacre by renouncing his knighthood, but he also invited the Indians to put their house in order. 'Do not mind the waves of the sea', he wrote in a letter to C. F. Andrews, 'but mind the leaks in your own vessel'.[9] All these statements of position by Tagore show clearly that he was transforming his universal humanistic ideals into an Indian debate. Ashis Nandy describes this Tagorean attitude as a denial of all forms of moral or cultural relativism. He underlines: 'A central theme in Tagore's reaffirmation of a moral universe was a universalism that denied moral and cultural relativism and endorsed a large, plural concept of India ... The first serious political thinker of modern India, Rammohun Roy, had refused to view the problems of India in isolation from the world, and this tradition was even more alive in Tagore's time.'[10] As such, following the tradition of the Indian Enlightenment of Rammohun Roy, Tagore clearly distinguished between 'patriotism' and 'nationalism'. For Tagore, patriotism was not a geopolitical or ideological concept. Being a patriot had to do with the spirit of the land and one's roots, whereas a nation was represented by political borders and mental ghettos. According to Nandy, in an interview with S. Gopalakrishnan,

> Tagore was a patriot. Patriotism means love for one's country – a sense of territoriality ... Patriotism is a form of territoriality – a certain emotional attachment to place of one's birth, the place where you have grown up, place which frames your earliest memories. Nationalism is different. Nationalism is not a sentiment. It is an ideology. It is based on the idea of that nation. Tagore believed

> that India was a country of communities. It was not a country of a nation. So, trying to build a nation in India was like an attempt to build a navy in Switzerland, that is what he wrote. Because nation and nationalism presume that you homogenise the population … my feeling is this that Tagore's hostility to nationalism came from the awareness that the nation state system and the idea of nation and nationality and nationalism were totally incongruent with Indian self-definition and went against the basic principle on which the Indic civilization as well as Indian unity as such is organised. So that is the background of Tagore's criticism of nationalism. That criticism was not lightweight. He believed in it strongly.[11]

Adopting a humanist view of nationhood, Tagore saw himself in the mirror of humanity. At the same time, he believed that the humiliation of being colonized can only be overcome by retaining one's pride in one's country. Tagore admits the following: 'Courage may be comforting or discomforting but it always invokes respect; away must be kept open in any state for the expression of heroism. In absence of such an opening, it finds expression in peculiar ways and its consequences become unthinkable.'[12] Undoubtedly, the formative years of the young Rabindranath and the moral and spiritual influence which he received from his surroundings gave him a sense of pride and self-confidence as a Bengali and a temperament of inclusiveness as an Indian. It was Tagore's process of opening up to an inclusive concept of India and the world that shaped his anti-nationalistic universalism. Tagore, therefore, gradually sought to transform anti-colonial dissent into a universal experience of harmony and interconnectedness among cultures. Searching rootedness in human beings, rather than what represented them politically, opened new doors of perception for Tagore to be in touch with the common humanity, which he called the 'Eternal Man'. Tagore's vision was assuredly premised on a belief in the 'unity of the soul' which left no space for a clash of individuals or cultures. 'It is not an abstract soul', wrote Tagore, 'but it is my own soul which I must realize in others.'[13] There are many common points in the 'personalist' of Tagore and that of a Christian non-violent humanist like Martin Luther King, Jr Though King was a self-declared follower of Mahatma Gandhi and his philosophy of non-violence, and he probably never read Tagore, his idea of 'cosmic companionship' was very close to Tagore's spiritual Universalist thinking. King deduced non-violence from the principle of 'personality', and he constructed his ideal of an inclusive society with reference to the ideas of 'personal God' and 'the sacredness of human personality'. For both Tagore and King, personal God was not a theocratic principle to whom one should obey without reason. They both considered this personal God as a lovable and a loving entity who had traced the arc of the universe and was both transcendent and immanent. In the case of Tagore, though he was not a Christian, his familiarity with the teachings of Jesus Christ and his friendship with Christians like C. F. Andrews opened new doors to religious personalism next to his readings of the *Upanishads*. Admittedly, both Tagore and King, each in their own way, also used the concept of 'personality' as an understanding of the human dignity. It is in this sense that Martin Luther King, Jr. apprehended the philosophy of personalism during his active years as the moral and political leader of the civil rights movement in America. This is what King wrote in his famous book, *Stride Toward Freedom*, 'This personal idealism remains today my basic philosophical position. Personalism's insistence that only personality – finite and infinite – is ultimately real strengthened me in two convictions: it gave me metaphysical and philosophical grounding for the idea of a personal God, and it gave me a metaphysical basis for the dignity and worth of all human personality.'[14]

Tagore was among the first in the twentieth century to search for a whole world of humanity with a grammar that carries its shared values. Tagore considered his universalism as creative, anti-uniformist and respectful of differences. He wrote in his essay, 'The Unity of Education',

> I must try to make it clear that uniformity is not unity; only those who are different can unite. Nations which wipe out the independence of other nations are the destroyers of interdependence. Imperialist nations swallow up other nations, python-like, and they call it unity. If the spiritual swallows up the material interest of man, the result cannot be called a synthesis of spirit and matter. The synthesis takes place only when they remain separate and yet unite. Only by admitting the individuality of men in matters in which they are separate can we arrive at their real unity in matters in which they are one.[15]

Clearly, Tagore was different from many of his contemporaries, in India and elsewhere, who believed in the uniqueness and superiority of their religion or culture. Specifically, Tagore was critical towards the nationalist impetus for cultural or racial supremacy. He saw the politics of the strongest and the fittest as the source of civilizational cannibalism. For him, this was the historical moment of the replacement of the concept of 'people' by that of 'nation'. Tagore argued:

> Nations live in an atmosphere of fear, greed and panic, due to the preying of one nation upon other [*sic*] for material wealth. Its civilisation is carnivorous and cannibalistic, feeding upon the blood of weaker nations. Its one idea is to thwart all greatness outside its boundaries. Never before were there such terrible jealousies, such betrayals of trust; all this is called patriotism, whose creed is politics.[16]

The nation, unlike the 'people' is, therefore, characterized by Tagore as an expression of 'moral blindness' and 'selfishness'. In other words, nationalism announces the end of common humanity. It destroys the public sphere and dissolves the cultural *sensus communis*. As such, from a Tagorean perspective, the challenge of nationalist politics is to maintain the link between the particular and the universal by highlighting and promoting a global space of deeds and words. However, the utopian construction of nationalism destroys this space with a violent intervention. Tagore was certainly very conscious about this, and what he feared mostly was violence done by one nation to another. Tagore observed nationalist societies as sites of power where there was an open invitation to violence.

Tagore's attention to the nationalist causes of violence was mainly focused on a continuous movement towards exclusion. 'Nationalism', wrote Tagore, 'is the training of a whole people for a narrow ideal.'[17] Tagore's rejection of nationalist violence stemmed from his belief that the very existence of a civilization is dependent on the proper understanding of the Other. However, his thoughts on nationalist violence can also be seen to raise issues with an imagined community. This is notably fictionalized by Tagore in his novel *Gora* (1910) in which the hero, who is a vehement Hindu nationalist, finds out that he is an orphan of Irish parents and not a Hindu. This is the end of his Hindu sectarianism and the beginning of his critique of all forms of communalism. 'Today I am free', says Gora, 'Today I have become an Indian-Bharatvarsha. In me there is no hostility towards any community, Hindu, Muslim or Christian. Today I belong to every community of this Bharatvarsha, I accept everyone's food as mine.'[18] What Tagore is trying to show the reader in *Gora* is that any individual from a certain religious or cultural background has a greater Universal Soul which invites him to reconcile with the Eternal Man. As Kaylan Chatterjee point out,

> that is why [Tagore] prepares for a smoother evolution of the hero by reclaiming him from his rigid position in religion and social philosophy. He is drawn out of his 'fortress', a term actually used by the author. After serving out a prison term, Gora has a growing disquiet of spirit and embarks on a mission to discover the 'greater India' by a typical act: journey and sojourn in the countless villages

> and rural communities of the vast country. A needed perspective is restored to his mind: the geo-political image of the motherland, a polity that is too pluralistic to support rigid theses. It is at this juncture that his 'father' reveals to him the truth about his birth in order to stop him, a *mlechcha*, from making the Hindu offerings at his funeral, for he (father) is afraid he is going to die soon. But this traumatic revelation does not make Gora a wreck and derelict because his journey and sojourn now have given him the country itself, greater, as he realises, than the 'fortress' of his own making ... The significant note here is that of re-birth. At the very moment of being caught in a limbo, of having to go nowhere, he finds a new habitation through a new baptism. At the same time as Hindu sanctums closed their doors against him, the vast country with its diversity is thrown open before him for a new quest, a new career, a new victory possibly.[19]

From Tagore's point of view, historical judgement takes a fallible stand within the pluralistic and syncretic civilizational framework. The most authentic goodness might leave the problems of a Tagorean hero unsolved, but the idea of a possible intercultural dialogue helps the characters to go on living with themselves within the dialogue of their own soul. After all, Tagore believes in the moral and spiritual dimensions of forgiveness which draw a line under past events and enable people to make a new start. Forgiveness, in other words, is not only the mode in which characters like Gora triumph over violent death recommended by sectarian and nationalistic ideologies, but it is the one miracle-working labour of the Universal Mind. As such, Tagore's multiple confrontations with the exclusivist and violent conceptions of nationalism in the east and the west encouraged him to think in terms of advocating a universal ethics. That is why, 'Tagore, once again, sought to assert the foundations of his country's complex identity so as to re-imagine India and the world – as well as India *in* the world – along open and non-sectarian lines. If ownership and territoriality were categories that needed transcending with respect to 'the nation', this was because Tagore's political philosophy was poised, in no uncertain terms, against the nation-state.'[20] His most severe critique of the idea of 'nation' came with his lectures on nationalism, published in 1917 as *Nationalism*. The first point to be made here is that Tagore defined 'the Nation' in terms of a machinery which is destroying the moral essence of the people. He wrote: 'A nation, in the sense of the political and economic union of a people, is that aspect which a whole population assumes when organized for a mechanical purpose.' Therefore, according to Tagore, the nation has replaced the society, where there was 'a spontaneous self-expression of man as a social being, [and] a natural regulation of human relationships, so that men can develop ideals of life in co-operation with one another'.[21] In the development of his argument about nationalism, Tagore also underlined the two dimensions of 'professionalism' and 'commercialism', which are closely related to modern utilitarian and bureaucratic modes of organizing the society.

According to Tagore, professionalism is the specialization of knowledge, which diminishes the task of the moral man.

> This history has come to a stage when the moral man, the complete man, is more and more giving way, almost without knowing it, to make room for the political and the commercial man, the man of the limited purpose. This process, aided by the wonderful progress in science, is assuming gigantic proportion and power, causing the upset of man's moral balance, obscuring his human side under the shadow of soulless organization. We have felt its iron grip at the root of our life, and for the sake of humanity we must stand up and give warning to all, that this nationalism is a cruel epidemic of evil that is sweeping over the human world of the present age, eating into its moral vitality.[22]

This simply means that Tagore saw nationhood and nationalism as dangerous enemies of the harmonious nature of the whole and at the same time for world peace. What Tagore saw as human nature was a fallible and fragile being, homo fragilis, who is fully aware of its incompleteness. In the eyes of Tagore, what this 'fragility' suggested was a historical need in mankind for relationship and love. He wrote in 'The Religion of Man':

> One may imagine that an individual who succeeds in disassociating himself from his fellows attains real freedom, inasmuch as all ties of relationship implied obligation to others. But we know that … it is true that in the human world only a perfect arrangement of interdependence gives rise to freedom. The most individualistic of human beings who own no responsibility are the savages who failed to attain their fullness of manifestation … only those maintain freedom … who have the power to cultivate mutual understanding and cooperation. The history of the growth of freedom is the history of the perfection of human relationships.[23]

As we have seen, Tagore saw nationalism as the expression of a civilization of power. Also, in the development of Tagore's argument about the nation and nationalism, we see the delusional aspect of such a society, which makes people think that they are loved and are free. In a letter to C. F. Andrews after his return from the United States, Tagore wrote:

> We must keep in mind that love of persons and love of ideas can be terribly egoistic, and that love can therefore lead to bondage instead of setting us free. It is constant sacrifice and service, which alone can loosen the shackles. We must not merely enjoy our love (whether personal or ideal) by contemplating its beauty and truth, but giving expression to it in our life's work.[24]

Whether one agrees or not with Tagore, his insistence on the connection between the creative capacity of the individual and its sociopolitical freedom remains very pertinent and relevant. Tagore, somehow, anticipated the contemporary critique of instrumental rationality, while remaining in the spiritual domain of the inner self.

The fact that Tagore rigorously underlined the emotional significance and the ethical importance of human cooperation shows that he was deeply concerned by a proto-totalitarian enslavement of human beings and their capacity to think. It is in a similar context that Tagore expressed his rage against Mahatma Gandhi. As reported by Michael Collins, In a letter sent to C. F. Andrews as early as July 1915, Tagore made the following striking claim: 'Only a moral tyrant like Gandhi can think that he has the dreadful power to make his ideas prevails the means of slavery.' In spite of the fact that it was Tagore himself who first gave Gandhi the name of Mahatma – the 'great soul'– he held deep-seated reservations about Gandhi's intentions. 'It is absurd', Tagore wrote, 'to think that you must create slaves to make your ideas free':

> There are men of ideas who make idols of their ideas and sacrifice humanity before their altars. But in my worship of ideas, I am not a worshipper of *Kali*. So, the only course left open to me when my fellow-workers fall in love with form and fail to have complete faith in idea, is to go and give my idea new birth and create new possibilities for it. This may not be a practical method, but possibly it is the ideal one.[25]

Nobody in or outside India could conclude that, despite its ups and downs, the Tagore–Gandhi relationship was not based on mutual respect. The real affinity between the two was strongly shaped around their separate efforts to affirm the primacy of the ethical in human civilization. Though not read and appreciated anymore by the present generation of Indians, Gandhi's *Hind Swaraj*, written in 1909, remains a groundbreaking critique of modern civilization. One obvious reading of *Hind Swaraj* is to consider it as an important work of political philosophy produced in the twentieth century. However, it would be difficult to make the same judgement about the philosophical and literary writings of Tagore. As Ashis Nandy argued,

> here lay [Tagore's] basic difference with Gandhi, to whom politics was a means of testing the ethics appropriate to our times and was therefore crucial to one's moral life … Everyone did not have to be an active politician, but everyone, Gandhi felt, had to work within a framework in which politics had a special place. What linked the two, was however their continuing attempts to reaffirm a moral universe within which one's politics and social ideology could be located … A central theme in Tagore's reaffirmation of a moral universe was an universalism that denied moral and cultural relativism and endorsed a large, plural concept of India.[26]

Tagore's disillusion and loss of faith in the Western civilization brought him closer to Gandhi in the last years of his life. He formulated his despair in his famous essay 'Crisis in Civilization':

> The spectre of a new barbarity strides over Europe, teeth bare and claws unconcealed in an orgy of terror … The spirit of violence dormant perhaps in the psychology of the West has roused itself and is ready to desecrate the spirit of Man … I look back on the stretch of past years and see the crumbling ruins of a proud civilization lying heaped as garbage out of history! And yet I shall not commit the grievous sin of losing faith in Man, accepting his present defeat as final.[27]

As we read again these words of Tagore, we realize that the dialogue between him and Gandhi was one of the most original and significant friendships of the twentieth century. As such, no one working on Tagore's thoughts and writings can ignore these compelling conversations. They constitute an unprecedented way of thinking about the moving boundaries of violence and non-violence in our world.

5

Tagore and Gandhi: Nobility of Spirit and Emancipation

Tagore and Gandhi met for the first time on 6 March 1915 at Santiniketan. Intriguingly, they were introduced to each other by a non-Indian, Charlie Andrews. Gandhi returned to India from South Africa on 9 January 1915 and one of his first wishes was to meet Rabindranath Tagore. The two men, who were known later to us as Gurudev and Mahatma, shared many values and ideas, but at the same time they were very different. 'In their relationship from 1915 to 1941,' argues Bindu Puri, 'they differed and argued about many things, such as the non-cooperation movement, nationalism and internationalism, the efficacy of *charkha* and the means for the attainment of *swaraj*.'[1] Gandhi stayed for a month at Santiniketan and familiarized himself with Tagore's ideas on education, art and interculturality. Though courteous, gentle and curious about each other's opinions concerning the British Raj and European culture, the differences and disagreements began to emerge. According to Shankar Bose, the

> meeting between the two men, both so firmly rooted in Indian culture, was a picture in contrast and they discussed many matters including Gandhi's favorite subject of dietetics. Gandhi maintained that for making puris good grains were converted into poison by frying the same in ghee or oil. Tagore, the lover of art and life, said that he had been eating puris all his life and they did him no harm.[2]

Other differences also became immediately clear when the two men started discussing the future of India and the prospects of self-determination. Today, when we look back at these two towering figures of modern India, we find the distinctions between them as expressions of the spirit of their time. As such, Krishna Dutta and Andrew Robinson are right to underline these differences between the two men as personality traits:

> The cherisher of beauty versus the ascetic; the artist versus the utilitarian; the thinker versus the man of action; the individualist versus the politician; the elitist versus the populist; the widely read, versus the narrowly-read; the modernist versus the reactionary; the believer in science versus the anti-scientist; the synthesiser of East and West versus the Indian chauvinist; the internationalist versus the nationalist; the traveller versus the stay-at-home; the Bengali versus the Gujarati; the scholarly Brahmin versus the merchant Vaishya … the fine flowing robes and beard versus the coarse loincloth and bald pate.[3]

Truly speaking, there is no black and no white in the Tagore–Gandhi debate. Gandhi was certainly more of a political animal and a less romantic person than Tagore. Also, he never had the time or the literary education to be a cultural globe-traveller like Tagore. However, all his life, he remained open to other cultures and to different traditions of thought. As he said famously, 'I do not want my house to be walled in on all sides and my windows to be stuffed. I want the culture of all lands to be blown about my house as freely as possible. But I refuse to be blown off my feet by any.'[4] Assuredly, Tagore had the feeling and the common sense that Gandhi would be a protector of his legacy at Visva-Bharati when he nominated him as the institution's life trustee. Let us not forget that both men were spiritual in character, though Gandhi appeared to be more ascetic than Tagore. However, Gandhi did not consider himself as an ascetic person. As he explained in *The Harijan*, in 1936,

> it is wrong to call me an ascetic. The ideals that regulate my life are presented for acceptance by mankind in general. I have arrived at them by gradual evolution. Every step was thought out, well-considered, and taken with the greatest deliberation. Both my continence and non-violence were derived from personal experience and became necessary in response to the calls of public duty. The isolated life I had to lead in South Africa whether as a householder, legal practitioner, social reformer, or politician, required, for the due fulfilment of these duties, the strictest regulation of sexual life and a rigid practice of nonviolence and truth in human relations, whether with my own countrymen or with the Europeans. I claim to be no more than an average man with less than average ability. Nor can I claim any special merit for such non-violence or continence as I have been able to reach with laborious research. I have not the shadow of a doubt that any man or woman can achieve what I have, if he or she would make the same effort and cultivate the same hope and faith.[5]

In other words, both Tagore and Gandhi were open to a fusion of eastern and western cultures, but most probably with different methodologies. Yet, Tagore's cultural universality and intercultural pragmatism went beyond simple phrases about others. Tagore thought in terms of a world house which was illuminated by multiple lamps. He argued: 'Let us be rid of all false pride and rejoice at any lamp being lit at any corner of the world, knowing that it is a part of the common illumination of our house.'[6] It is true that Tagore never portrayed himself as an English author, but it is also correct to say that he refused to see the rejection of British colonialism as a glory for Bengali culture and Indian heritage. The following lines capture his mindset limpidly: 'We have seen the influence of eastern art on European paintings, but that has not spelt doom for the western art and culture', therefore, how would denying European culture, 'necessarily reinforce the glory of our heritage?'[7] Undoubtedly, both Tagore and Gandhi had supreme self-confidence in their respective task for helping Indians to self-realize themselves around the world. However, Tagore did not consider the integration of Indian culture into the project of universalism as a political project. Despite his rare appearances in Calcutta, following the Proclamation of Partition in July 1905 and composition of a song which was adopted as an anthem of protest, Tagore's suspicions towards Indian politicians turned in later years into deep antipathies for politics in general. However, though Tagore was not a political philosopher, he had a clear conception of the state and society. Tagore placed society above the state and used to say that the heart of the people is where the responsibility for their welfare lies. In one of his rare political pamphlets entitled 'Our Swadeshi Samaj', Tagore developed the idea of social empowerment against political power. Tagore defined political power as an act of conquest and subjugation. The concept of political conquest was interpreted by the poet as *Sarkar* or government. Tagore observed a substantial difference between the concept of *Sarkar* as domination and *Samaj* as organization of social forces. 'Today', affirmed Tagore, 'we are striving, of our own accord, to place in the hands of the *Sarkar* the whole duty of our *Samaj*.'[8]

As a matter of fact, Tagore's pluralist approach to the question of *Swadeshi Samaj* went hand in hand with his emphasis on the idea of the welfare of the people in India. However, at this level of discussion, Tagore was more concerned by individual liberties than by the political sovereignty, incarnated by the state. Therefore, Tagore had a critical eye on all politicians because he believed that a large part of national life was ignored by politicians. 'Politicians', he argued, 'move blindly and mechanically and lack real human sensitivity to the actual needs of life and the country.'[9] According to Tagore, society in India was not dependent on political rulers but was in accordance with the duties and responsibilities accepted by the people. He affirmed: 'Hindu *Dharma* has always shown the way for every householder to transcend the narrowness of home or parish and relate himself to the universal.'[10]

It follows that Tagore saw the well-balanced social arrangement as a vital power of every civilization. Hence, the overriding need for Tagore was not to fall back on some pre-established conception of society. From his point of view, politics was for the sake of plurality. For Tagore, every culture, including Indian culture, could survive by forging a plural space of interchange. Tagore underlined clearly:

> The inmost creed of India is to find the one in the many, unity in diversity. India does not admit difference to be conflict, nor does she espy an enemy in every stranger. So she repels none, destroys none, and strives to find a place for all in a vast social order. She acknowledges every path and recognizes greatness wherever she finds it. Since India has this genius for unification, we do not have to fear imaginary enemies. We may look forward to our own expansion as the final result of each new struggle. Hindu and Buddhist, Muslim and Christian shall not die fighting on Indian soil; here they will find harmony. That harmony will not be non-Hindu; on the contrary, it will be peculiarly Hinduistic. And however cosmopolitan the several limbs may be, the heart will still be the heart of India.[11]

As we can see, more than many Indian politicians of his time, Tagore had a clear conception of society and the state. This is a major point that we need to have in mind when reading letters and debates between Tagore and Gandhi. According to Sabyasachi Bhattacharya,

> Rabindranath Tagore's experience as an active participant in the swadeshi movement following the partition of Bengal (1905) may have sensitised the poet to the limitations of the pre-Gandhian Congress and its politics. He saw, perhaps before his countrymen, that Gandhi promised to give an altogether new turn to the Indian struggle for freedom. Mohandas Karamchand Gandhi of South African fame might have sent his Phoenix School students to Tagore's Santiniketan because he saw that something was under way in that remote corner of Bengal, which shared some traits with his own endeavour and philosophy.[12]

Tagore followed the Calcutta sessions of the Indian National Congress, and this is how he learned about Gandhi's *satyagraha* campaign in South Africa. As a matter of fact, Charlie Andrews talked to Tagore about his journey to Durban and his meeting with Gandhi in 1913. All this to say that Tagore strongly believed in the 'spiritual force' and the 'fearless courage' of Gandhi. Yet admiring the man did not mean that he necessarily approved of his methods. Gandhi's *satyagraha* campaign directed against the Rowlatt Act of March 1919 and his request for Tagore's support received a cold response from Tagore. He wrote the following to Gandhi on 12 April 1919:

> Power in all its forms is irrational; - it is like the horse that drags the carriage blindfolded. The moral element in it is only represented in the man who drives the horse. Passive resistance is a force which is not necessarily moral in itself; it can be used against truth as well as for it. The danger inherent in all force grows stronger when it is likely to gain success, for then it becomes temptation. I know your teaching is to fight against evil by the help of good. But such a fight is for heroes and not for men led by impulses of the moment. Evil on one side naturally begets evil on the other, injustice leading to violence and insult to vengefulness. Unfortunately, such a force has already been started, and either through panic or through wrath our authorities has shown us the claws whose sure effect is to drive some of us into the secret path of resentment and others into utter demoralization.[13]

Tagore's letter had no impact on the mutual relation of confidence and friendship which existed between the two men. Yet, as time passed and Gandhi was more successful in his non-violent struggle, the debate and the exchange of letters between the two men became more intellectual and less concentrated on everyday politics. As Bhattacharya declares,

> the most remarkable thing about the intellectual exchange between Gandhi and Tagore is the high philosophical plane to

which they elevated a political debate, and the extent to which each of them – one holding the highest degree of political power in the sub-continent and the other as the pinnacle of intellectual eminence – was willing to learn from each other … [The two men debated central questions like] What is the role in politics of a poet or an intellectual disengaged from active politics? What are the limits of the individual's right to think and act on his own, when such thoughts or actions are in conflict with prescriptions and proscriptions emanating from a collective entity like the nation or the state? Is there any value higher than the free and rational exercise of one's mind? What are the limits of nationalism and are there values higher than nationalism?[14]

Indeed, Tagore refused to see the Gandhian approach to *swaraj* as a true battle for the spirit. Truly speaking, Tagore felt ill at ease about a national movement which had for objective to be in control of the state. Even though Gandhi understood *swaraj* primarily as the moral autonomy of the individual and not as an art of state-building, to Tagore individual freedom needed to be protected against any forms of institutionalized communities and collectives. Therefore, Tagore had no interest in a non-violent struggle for *swaraj* which was not at the same time a 'swaraj of the mind'. He wrote in his famous essay 'The Call of Truth':

> As everywhere else, swaraj in this country has to find its basis in the mind's unfoldment, in knowledge, in scientific thinking, and not in shallow gestures. It does not make sense that we would attain this swaraj by plying the spinning-wheel a brief while … The Mahatma has declared war against the tyranny of the machine which is oppressing the world. Here we are all under his banner. But we cannot accept as our ally in the fight the slave mentality that is at the root of all the misery and indignity in our national life. That, indeed, is our real enemy and through its defeat alone can swaraj within and without come to us.[15]

Tagore did not analyse *swaraj* as an end in itself. On the contrary, he believed that the moral value of *swaraj* was dependent on the individual self rather than the collective self. That is to say, while extending his anti-nationalist sentiments, Tagore was fully conscious of his role as an intellectual authority who questioned Indian political reality *à la* Socrates next to Gandhi's moral leadership. He wrote:

> Alien government in India is a kind of chameleon. Today it is seen in the guise of the Englishman, tomorrow it may take the form of some other foreigner, and the following day, its malignity unabated, it will bear the semblance of our countrymen. We may try to hunt down the monster of alien rule with lethal weapons, but it will baffle us every time by changing its skin and complexion. Only when we feel within us that our country exists, that is real, will the maya recede.[16]

Looking at these words, one can suggest that Tagore assumed the mantle of a philosopher who had the task to dissipate the illusions of the Indian people. This Tagorean viewpoint clearly defined a point of difference with Gandhi, for whom, 'the individual self could not become morally autonomous or free without recognizing his or her supreme moral duty to take cognizance of, engage in and resolve conflicts with hostile others'.[17] This major disagreement between Tagore and Gandhi was later reinforced by their dispute over the non-cooperation movement and the adoption of the charkha. However, all those who knew Gandhi and Tagore well qualified the exchange of ideas between the two men as a 'noble debate' and an 'august dispute'.[18] We need to admit that the debate between Tagore and Gandhi was deeply empathetic and had a projective dimension in the life in the Indian society. In short, Tagore and Gandhi inaugurated a culture of dialogue in India, which was more than a simple act of conversing or criticizing one another. They started a culture of dialogue which had in essence a kaleidoscopic vision of Indian social reality. While transcending the numerous differences which they pointed at in the exchange of letters, both Tagore and Gandhi tried to have an empathetic understanding of their common world. To be sure, what the conversations between the two men show us is a sense of urgency to understand the historical event in which they find themselves beyond a mere monistic logicality. This trend of thinking was premised upon the idea that even when their modes of approach were different, their intentionality remained the same. As Sabyasachi Bhattacharya underlines,

> where the two differed was when Gandhi goes on to say that 'when there is war, the poet lays down the lyre' ... Tagore's plea to Gandhi was that at no time should the poet 'lay down his lyre', or the scholar his books for the sake of *swaraj*: 'its foundation is in the mind, which with its diverse powers and its confidence in these powers, goes on all the time creating swaraj for itself.'[19]

Consequently, Gandhi's debate with Tagore was an instance of his philosophy of non-violence. As for Tagore, his situation of intellectual marginality, as the sage of Santiniketan, never did his intercultural mode of thinking and living. Marginality is usually referred to as a personality that is isolated in a society and is in search of an opportunity to take roots in a dominant discourse. However, in Tagore's case, it is quite the opposite. Tagore did not try to fit only in one of the cultures to which he was exposed. He tried to fit comfortably on the edge, in the margins of each culture, by keeping his critical distance from all of them, either Bengali, Indian or English. This intercultural in-betweenness placed Tagore in a form of constructive marginality, where he was able to move easily and powerfully between these different cultural traditions, acting appropriately and feeling at home in each. This is where the essential difference between Gandhi and Tagore resides. The former has a compassionate and non-violent sense of belonging to India, while the latter is an intercultural Indian with a universal sense of belonging. We can find the best example of such a differentiation in the letter that Gandhi wrote to Tagore in

April 1918, asking him not to travel and remain in India during his non-violent campaign. Gandhi wrote: 'We are on the threshold of a mighty change in India. I would like all the pure forces to be physically in the country during the process of her new birth. If therefore you could at all find rest anywhere in India, I would ask you and Mr. Andrews to remain in the country.'[20] It is not a secret to anyone that despite his friendship for Gandhi, Tagore had severe doubts about Gandhi's non-cooperation movement. These doubts had nothing to do with the nature of Gandhian struggle, since they were expressions of Tagore's intellectual marginality. Therefore, Tagore's strong sense of caring for and sharing with other human beings (and not necessarily only with Indians) as citizens of human history preceded all forms of national sense of belonging. As such, Tagore certainly gave voice to the elements of solidarity and interconnectedness which underpinned Gandhi's all-encompassing non-violent struggle for emancipation, but he found difficult to judge his own actions as part of a national history which did not call forth a common fate with the British. We can say, then, that for Tagore the discovery of this common fate was a product of his marginality as a poet–philosopher. His reflections on the non-cooperation movement in May 1921, published in the Calcutta journal *Modern Review*, expressed his downheartedness with the call to boycott government schools. He argued the following:

> The idea of non-cooperation is political asceticism. Our students are bringing their offering of sacrifices to what? Not to a fuller education, but to non-education. It has at its back a fierce joy of annihilation which at best is asceticism, and at its worst is that orgy of frightfulness in which the human nature, losing faith in the basic reality of normal life, finds a disinterested delight in an unmeaning devastation as has been shown in the late war and on other occasions which came nearer to us. No, in its passive moral form is asceticism and in its active moral form is violence … I say again and again that I am a poet, that I am not a fighter by nature.

> I would give everything to be one with my surroundings. I love my fellow beings and I prize their love. Yet I have been chosen by destiny to ply my boat there where the current is against me. What irony of fate is this that I should be preaching cooperation of cultures between East and West on this side of the sea just at the moment when the doctrine of non-cooperation is preached on the other side?[21]

For Tagore, non-violence was not a product of *swaraj*, but the outcome of a broader view of humanity as a whole. Furthermore, Tagore did not believe that Indians could become a country of non-violent individuals only by burning the British clothes, wearing the Khadi and following Gandhi. The criticism addressed to Gandhi and his followers was pointed at the absence of a rational discourse and an extensive use of moral language in place of the economic in the Swadeshi movement. Writing against the cult of the charkha, Tagore asserted: 'Simply by turning the charkha, weaving homespun yarn and holding grave discourses, we shall not be able to project the realization of what swaraj means. India as a whole must first be made true in a concrete form in some corner of the land, and then alone shall we begin to understand, by direct experience, the value of self-determination.'[22] Once again, Tagore's marginal position, as a poet and philosopher, made it difficult for him to join the Indian crowd and spin and burn British clothes without putting on his Socratic mask and asking questions. Tagore maintained that obeying without questioning was a way to accept the process of instrumentalization of *swaraj*. His answer to Gandhi's idea of *swaraj* was disobedience. 'We have been ordered to burn foreign cloth,' he wrote, 'I, for one, am unable to obey. First, because I believe it to be my duty to fight the habit of blind obedience. Secondly, I feel that the cloth to be burnt is not mine, it belongs to people who are sorely in need of it.'[23] Gandhi's response to Tagore's criticism was his famous article 'The Great Sentinel' written on 13 October 1921. He wrote,

> The spinning wheel is the thing which all must turn in the Indian clime for the transition stage at any rate and the vast majority must for all time. It was our love of foreign cloth that ousted the wheel from its position of dignity. Therefore, I consider it a sin to wear foreign cloth. I must confess I do not draw a sharp or any distinction between economics and ethics … I venture to suggest to the Poet that the clothes I ask him to burn must be and are his. If they had to his knowledge belonged to the poor or the ill-clad, he would long ago have restored to the poor what was theirs. In burning *my* foreign clothes, I burn my shame.[24]

It goes without saying that Gandhi was raising the question of self-sufficiency, while Tagore was suggesting to the Indians in general and members of the Indian Congress Party in particular to see the problem more broadly and in universal terms. We should not forget that Tagore's impulse towards the non-cooperation movement was more universal, rather than being concentrated on a specific Indian problem. Thus, Tagore's orientation towards Indian life experience was based on an understanding of other cultures as different experiences of the same shared life. In other words, Tagore's territory of plurality could emerge despite political and anthropological differences between Indians and the British. However, Tagore believed that Indians could not arrive at this moment of plurality if they did not consider it as a never-ending quest for excellence and exemplarity.

For Tagore, this sense of exemplarity existed not because of the awareness of similarities among Indians but because of the dissimilarities and differences between them and others (including their enemies). So, the theoretical framework for Tagore in his dialogue with Gandhi was 'many voices, one humanity'. However, if the Gandhi–Tagore controversy was a successful dialogue, it had to do with the fact that both men believed that violence can never be legitimate, and it should be fought by Truth and Beauty. Both Tagore and Gandhi accepted the fact that human beings have the moral and spiritual ability to bring humaneness out of the inhumane, as they can bring beauty out of ugliness and peace out of war. Even so, the debate between Gandhi and Tagore was constructed around this one central point of 'the public use of reason'. For Tagore, the public use of reason by Indians was the condition of a critical-minded India. Therefore, Tagore was concerned with moving the Indian subject out of the context of its nationalist heteronomy and into the context of autonomy. What Tagore's argument shows us is that education is a way of orienting one's mind towards the common judgement that we share with others. Therefore, from Tagore's point of view, the most pressing question was how to preserve – not in theory, but concretely – the courage of each Indian to form and defend a personal judgement. For Tagore, thinking critically was essentially an attitude of the mind, but also a moral orientation. This brings us to Tagore's relation between life and thought. Tagore was convinced that thinking was a great asset for human beings. That is why he believed that thinking freedom and freedom of thinking went together. However, he also argued that there could be no real freedom without a life of the mind. Tagore wrote:

> At this dawn of the world's awakening, if our own national endeavour holds no intimations of a universal message, the poverty of our spirit will be laid piteously bare … Universal humanity has sent uș its urgent call. Let our mind answer in its own language. Formerly, we were engrossed in discovering and pointing out the faults and shortcomings of our rulers. Now that we bent on dissociating our politics from dependence, are we to continue that recital to feed our policy of boycott? The dust of angry passion will only obscure the greater world from our view.[25]

All his life, Tagore had a view of the greater world. Above all, the Tagore–Gandhi debate helps us to appreciate the value that Tagore gave to the nobility of spirit. As such, Tagore saw the overcoming of the colonial mind in India as a work of historical consciousness. Therefore, for him, freedom could only emerge in a certain social-historical situation that was accompanied by self-awareness of human beings. If Tagore was among us today, he would continue to believe that we cannot be at the level of our idea of true (true?) freedom if we continue to create slaves. Crucially, for Tagore, humanity had to realize itself in its capacity to think and to live freely. This is where, among many other ideas, we can find the relevance of Rabindranath Tagore.

Conclusion: A Philosopher of Decency and Dignity

The best-known authors are not the most widely read. Rabindranath Tagore verifies this rule. For more than half a century, Tagore the philosopher was concealed by the man with the white beard and a prophetic look. Bengal has now run out of people who knew Tagore personally, but Bengalis continue to look up to Tagore as a poet and a writer who shaped their modern identity and culture. However, for an author who is fetishized as an inescapable component of Bengali popular culture, his legacy as a philosopher is minimized, not to say forgotten. According to Priyam Marik in his article for *The Telegraph*,

> for a people that can never get enough of Tagore anecdotes and memorabilia, Bengalis pay little to no attention to some of the most fundamental aspects of Tagore. First, Tagore, the philosopher, whose faith in universal fraternity as a counterpoint to narrow and divisive nationalism has been largely overlooked for decades. In the contemporary political climate, when nationalism has emerged as a hot-button issue, Bengalis seem least interested in reminding their fellow Indians of how Tagore believed that 'patriotism (used interchangeably with nationalism here) cannot be our final spiritual shelter, [for] my refuge is humanity' ... Second comes Tagore, the caricatured mystic, whose magnetic hold over Bengal initially found massive resonance, and then, almost as much ridicule across much of the rest of the world. Following his acceptance of the Nobel Prize in Literature for *Gitanjali* in 1913, Tagore rocketed to fame as Germany's first best-selling author, was hailed as a cult-figure

> in Spain, and accumulated considerable renown in Russia, Japan, Latin America as well as the US. However, within a few frivolous years, Tagore's global standing diminished considerably, with the Argentine writer Jorge Luis Borges calling him a 'hoaxer of good faith … a Swedish invention'. In the UK, where Tagore's translations into English had once won over the likes of William Butler Yeats and Ezra Pound, Tagore was quickly reduced to an Oriental sage whose literature (along with his beard) evoked more amusement than admiration.[1]

Tagore was neither a system builder like Kant, Hegel or Schelling, nor a mystic, guru or a great seer of Truth like Ramakrishna, Vivekananda or even Krishnamurti. He was rather a creator and an educator with a world view (*Weltanschauung*). He represented a nobility of spirit that not everybody in India could attain. This was expressed by a penetrating knowledge of humanities and civilizations, which not too many individuals in India or Asia were ever likely to have. More significantly, Tagore stood out as a key witness to a time when the most profound evil had returned to the Earth. The rise of nationalism and sectarianism had led to a clash of fraternities, followed by the eclipse of human civilization. Rabindranath Tagore, thus, became the geographer of the human soul, torn between empathy and revolt. For this pilgrim of the human soul, brotherhood alone could answer for evil and restore the spirit of humanity to its nobility. Also, Tagore was one of the very few intellectuals of the twentieth century who placed friendship at the centre of his metaphysical and aesthetic vision of the world. He was one of the very few, indeed, because in his century, friendship was rejected by all political ideologies.

As it was discussed previously, Tagore considered God and Nature as friends of Man. This was not a matter of bland sentimentalism. It was a search for the depths of the human soul, beyond the Promethean illusion of modern civilization. Tagore recognized the moral values of God and Nature in the process of the metaphysical and aesthetic education of mankind. This education was at the centre of the fullest self-development of human beings as a search for a bond of unity. In this process of increasing concern with universalism, he expressed his disappointment with provincialism, self-centredness and sectarianism of human beings and cultures which had lost their moral compass. It is precisely the search for this moral compass and this experience of empathy in the midst of human cultures that points to the supreme value of friendship in Tagore's work. A prerequisite for the construction of a political community, the value of friendship can be found at every stage of Tagore's life and work. It was also a decisive way for Tagore to condemn all forms of violence while searching for non-violence in the contribution of cultures to a universal humanism. Tagore sought empathy and non-violence in the geography of the human soul. He wrote in 1906:

> The soul is our spiritual life, and it contains our infinity within it. It has an impulse that urges our consciousness to break through the dimly lighted walls of anima life where our turbulent passions fight to gain mastery in a narrow enclosure. Though, like animals, man is dominated by his self, he has an instinct that struggles against it, like the rebel life within a seed that breaks through the dark prison, bringing out its flag of freedom to the realm of light … Our sages saw no end to the dignity of the human spirit which found its consummation in the Supreme Spirit itself. Any limited view of man would be false. He could not be merely Citizen or Patriot, for neither city nor country, nor for the matter the bubble called the world, could contain his eternal soul.[2]

Thus, Tagore's adventure in the region of the soul is marked by the cry for greater freedom of conscience. Tagore's message here would be to spare every human being the humiliation of conscience. This is the absurdity of the human condition represented by the absence of the search for a higher life. Tagore asserted:

> I cannot admit that there is anything in man's higher life which is good only in a particular geographic latitude. It is not true that we must take refuge in meekness because we are weak, or that we want righteousness only as a convenient cloak for hiding our poverty. Ideals preached by the great personalities of the world need for their acceptance more steady courage, perfect training and power of sacrifice than what is needed to make good our school-learnt lessons on the profits of competition and the carnage of a hungry nationalism thriving on human flesh.[3]

Thus, in a civilization that does not ordain any fundamental values, Tagore suggests the maturity of the soul through self-restraint and self-dedication. For Tagore, this is one of the highest forms of human friendship in the world.

The great lesson of Tagore's creative life is that art creates friendship among civilizations. For Tagore, the wholeness of Man originates from art. Initially, this where and how Tagore saw the true and complete personality of modern Europe. As he said,

> we in India see the European, where he is learned, where he is masterful, where he is busily constructive in his trade and politics, but not where he is artistically creative. That is why modern Europe has not been revealed to us in her complete personality, but only in her intellectual power and utilitarian activities; and therefore, she has only touched our intellect and evoked our utilitarian ambitions.[4]

What Tagore showed us was that the modern civilization is too talkative since it has lost the capacity of loving silently. For him, philosophical friendship came with the silence of thinking and the love of wisdom (*philo-sophos*). Tagore saw art and philosophy as internal voices of friendship. He knew well that neither of these could turn into the evil forces of sectarianism and communalism. Tagore saw the whole world, and not only Indian civilization, as the Man's true home on Earth. As a result, he believed that friendship created among civilizations, through art, philosophy and spirituality, protected Man's poetic dwelling on Earth. Tagore's western tour, during which he preached the imperatives of friendship between east and west, was followed by an article in the *Modern Review* which deserves to be quoted extensively:

> All humanity's greatest is mine. The infinite personality of man (as the Upanishads say) can only come from the magnificent harmony of all human races. My prayer is that I may represent the co-operation of all the peoples of the world. For India, unity is truth, and division evil. Unity is that which embraces and understands everything; consequently, it cannot be attained through negation. The present attempt to separate our spirit from that of the Occident is a tentative of spiritual suicide ... The present age has been dominated by the Occident, because the Occident had a mission to fulfil. We of the Orient should learn from the Occident. It is regrettable, of course, that we had lost the power of appreciating our own culture, and therefore did not know how to assign Western culture to its right place. But to say that it is wrong to co-operate with the West is to encourage the worst form of provincialism and can produce nothing but intellectual indigence. The problem is a world problem. No nation can find its own salvation by breaking away from others. We must all be saved, or we must all perish together.[5]

Rabindranath Tagore always considered the artist as the animator of the *cosmic friendship* among human cultures. He was aware that only the artist, with its vision of the invisible, could see the statue in the stone or the poem in the soul. So, Tagore did value art as necessary for the soul's journey towards the Universal Man. Only in the eyes of Tagore, a painting or a poem represent the highest idea of Man. He knew that 'the word own Man' (*Das Wort hat den Menschen*) as Heidegger would say a few decades later.[6] As such, Tagore learnt to listen to words and to respect them, so that he can find his *home* and his *cosmic friendship* in their mystery. He wrote:

> When mankind learnt to preserve language through the written word, the area of contact between minds was extended. Spoken words do not go far. They get lost in course of time, and often become distorted as they pass from mouth to mouth. But the written word crosses oceans and mountains and is still unchanged. Every man may thus gain the thinking of countless others. This is not all. The written word goes beyond uniting the minds of living men alone; it removes the barriers between the minds of today and the minds of those who belonged to a remote past. This great contact between thoughts has created what is called civilization. What is civilization but a state of union in which the strength of each individual adds power to all and the power of all fortifies the individual?[7]

'Every thought begins with a poem' (*Toute pensée commence par un poème*),[8] said the French philosopher Alain. Tagore's philosophical journey began with a poetic act. The fact remains that only Tagore could have seen the friendship of the world under the sign of poetry. Under his pen, the word became a tool in the service of the heritage of the nobility of the world. He wrote in poem no. 12 of the *Gitanjali*: 'The traveller has to knock at every alien door to come to his own, and one has to wander through all the outer worlds to reach the innermost shrine at the end.'[9] We can see in this poem how Tagore beautifully establishes the spiritual link between everyday individual existence and the dignity of spiritual transcendence. Tagore's art in general, from his early poems to his paintings later in life, cannot be viewed in isolation and separate from his spiritual journey to the joy of the universal. This is where the tragic vision of the ontological fragility of Man joined the beauty of creation, and the grand myths of the modern world (progress, democracy, conquest etc.) obscured humanity's view of the world.

Tagore was undoubtedly the visionary genius who stood against the world where only the spirit of conquest remained. He was the conscience of a world where great civilizational changes were underway and where the greatest danger threatening humanity's cultural heritage was the rise of insignificance and meaninglessness. Tagore was among those Indian intellectuals who championed the idea of freedom against the meaningless and individualist insight that one can choose to do what one wants. As Tagore saw it, the idea of freedom was not only a process of self-realization and self-liberation (as in the Gandhian *swaraj*) but also a close association with the concept of common humanity. Tagore argued on behalf of freedom as self-restriction, because of the sense of belonging of the individual *to* a common humanity, as opposed to the individualist freedom *from* common humanity. As Tagore declared,

> freedom may be attained through the bonds of discipline, through the sacrifice of personal inclinations. Freedom is a profit which may be gained only if you lay an adequate capital of self-restriction … [But] we still submit to the bondage of all kinds of social restrictions, but the emancipation which was the object is no longer in our view. We have forgotten the ideal, we have lost all sense of the grandeur of our striving, what remains is the impotence of blind habit.[10]

Tagore puts forward the perspective of the enlarged way of thinking, which transcends all the mental ghettos, either religious or political, which put in danger the process of emancipation. What Tagore wrote reminds us of a lecture by Hannah Arendt on *Freedom and Politics*, where she argued the following: 'We are inclined to believe that freedom begins where politics ends, because we have seen that freedom disappeared where politics became endless and limitless. The less politics, so it seems, the more freedom.'[11] Tagore remained skeptical of party politics all his life, maybe because he believed that where the idea of freedom could serve as a unifying principle, binding all Indians in a common action for spiritual transcendence, politics failed to be the structural idea of a syncretic collective. What

Tagore understood by a comprehensive public sphere was a space of reasoning, argumentation and dialogue. That is why, in his lectures on nationalism, he rejected an unquestioned community that he specified under the concept of 'political civilization'. He asserted:

> The political civilization which has sprung up from the soil of Europe and is overrunning the whole world, like some prolific weed, is based upon exclusiveness. It is always watchful to keep at bay the aliens or to exterminate them. It is carnivorous and cannibalistic in its tendencies, it feeds upon the resources of other peoples and tries to swallow their whole future. It is always afraid of other races achieving eminence, naming it as a peril, and tries to thwart all symptoms of greatness outside its own boundaries, forcing down races of men who are weaker, to be eternally fixed in their weakness. Before this political civilization came to its power and opened its hungry jaws wide enough to gulp down great continents of the earth, we had wars, pillages, changes of monarchy and consequent miseries, but never such a sight of fearful and hopeless voracity, such wholesale feeding of nation upon nation, such huge machines for turning great portions of the earth into mincemeat, never such terrible jealousies with all their ugly teeth and claws ready for tearing open each other's vitals. This political civilization is scientific, not human. It is powerful because it concentrates all its forces upon one purpose, like a millionaire acquiring money at the cost of his soul. It betrays its trust, it weaves its meshes of lies without shame, it enshrines gigantic idols of greed in its temples, taking great pride in the costly ceremonials of its worship, calling this patriotism.[12]

As such, Tagore's attempt to maintain the distinction between a civilization without ethical ideals and a history with 'a moral spirit of combination'[13] was the expression of his strong commitment to an intersubjective view of political creation. As a matter of fact, Tagore's stress on the centrality of the public use of reason as a guarantor of individual freedom goes hand in hand with his idea of a cosmopolitan and universalist human history. However, perhaps most crucially, Tagore's call on us to recognize that plurality is basic to the possibility of every community and civilization against the ideological temptations to short-circuit the syncretic character of mankind finds its truest expression in his famous *Hymn to India*:

> Awake my mind, gently awake
> in this holy place of pilgrimage
> on the shore of this vast sea of humanity that is India.
> Here I stand with arms outstretched to hail man,
> man divine in his own image,
> and sing to his glory in notes glad and free.
> These mountains rapt in meditation,
> these plains with rivers winding like rosaries,
> behold this earth that is ever holy–
> on the shore of this vast sea of humanity
> that is India.[14]

Tagore's account of plurality and universality was in important ways precisely not of a pre-established similarity among members of humanity. In sum, Tagore's claim to a common world was a search for a shared Truth by all human cultures and civilizations. He had no intention to measure the greatness of mankind by its material resources, but he bet on India's nobility of spirit. In his letter of May 1921 to Charlie Andrews, he wrote:

> That the measure of man's greatness is in his material resources is a gigantic illusion casting its shadow over the present-day world – it is an insult to man. It lies in the power of the materially weak to save the world from this illusion and India, in spite of her penury and humiliation can afford to come to the rescue of humanity.[15]

Perhaps we should accept the fact that, in spite of his severe critique of the materialist and instrumentalist west, the rooted universalism of Tagore guided him towards the acceptance of the spirit of modernity. Tagore can perhaps be recognized as an Indian representative of the *Weltliteratur*, who understood and created his poetry of the same breath as that of his Universalist humanism. Therefore, rather than feeling hostility and alienation to a different culture, Tagore's proximity to the Goethian spirit of *Weltliteratur* encouraged a profound humanistic spirit deployed with generosity and hospitality. After all, Tagore's sense of plurality in culture and in politics was rooted firmly within worldliness, by articulating a philosophical view that envisaged the 'Other' not as an object of exclusion or subordination but as an object of empathy (*Einfühlung*). In short, Tagore invited us to resist all forms of opaque and non-transparent authority which unleashed enormous violence upon our world. In other words, Tagore's critical effort of mapping empathetic universalism constituted an intellectual engagement which involved both a humanistic acknowledgement of rationality and a critical dethroning of instrumental forms of rationality. Tagore explained his disappointment with the utilitarian aspects of England in his famous *Diary of a Westward Voyage* written in 1924–5:

> England's need for India is entirely utilitarian. To view anything from the standpoint of utility is to view with the idea of 'getting'. In this 'getting' there is not a suspicion of 'not-getting'; that is why it cannot be said that there is truth in this seeing. Because the essential truth is lacking in this seeing there is no feeling of wonder, no reverence. A relationship of necessity is totally a relationship of taking; the greed is there, but there is no joy. The relationship that is real is a mingling of both receiving and giving; for, it is joy that sets the mind free. This is why one is so aware of the extraordinary lack of generosity in the individual Englishman towards an Indian. This is not said as a complaint, for this is inevitable under the circumstances. The India that England's greed possessed is what the soul of England has lost.[16]

Tagore's *Diary*, written on a ship, S.S. *Cracovia*, like Mahatma Gandhi's *Hind Swaraj*, is certainly more poetic because of Tagore's literary background. However, it seems that the two great minds of India in the twentieth century were both searching for moments of truthfulness and peace of mind in their confrontation with the cult of success in Western civilization. As Tagore underlined in his own writing,

> this excitability in the frantic race for success is continually raising whirlwinds on the Western horizon ... In the path of success cleverness has no patience, it knows no restraint; the faster it moves by distorting its arms and legs, the more wonderful the jugglery appears to us, so that the tempo in this wizard-civilization is so hastened in every direction that the mind of man has no time to feel ashamed of its untruth, or to fear the danger of a suicidal death.[17]

It is worth mentioning that for Tagore, outward progress, as it was understood in the west, was of secondary importance in comparison with the *dharmic* essence of Man which gave him inward progress, independent of any non-self-realized and self-supported agency. Conceptualized as an ethical form of resistance, *dharma* in Tagore's work can be described as a heightened form of intellectual awareness and moral maturity. It is a process of intense reflection on the inward progress of life in contradistinction from the historical progress of Man. Tagore observed the following in his essay on *Nationalism*: 'You have to judge progress according to its aim. A railway train makes its progress towards the terminus station – it is a movement. But a full-grown tree has no definite movement of that kind. Its progress is the inward progress of life. It lives, with its aspiration towards light tingling in its leaves and creeping in its silent sap.'[18]

Tagore acknowledged that Truth and Beauty could spontaneously bring human beings close to Nature, God and the Universal Man and facilitate their inward progress. However, at the same time, he was quite aware of the fact that no harmony could exist without the silence and solitude of the creative mind and far from the fury of the masses. He wrote to Romain Rolland in February 1924:

> I myself have a kind of civil war constantly going on my own nature between my personality as a creative artist who necessarily must be solitary and that as an idealist who must realize himself through works of a complex character needing a large field of cooperation with a large body of men … I suppose a proper rhythm is possible to be attained in which both may be harmonised, and my work in the heart of the crowd may find its grace through the touch of breath that comes from the solitude of the creative mind."[19]

Tagore, for one, did not enjoy his loneliness, but he knew that he could not develop his Socratic soul without a particular art of living. In a letter to his friend, Rani Mahalanobis, he wrote: 'Perhaps my true nature is of solitude – the impact of company does not give it any strength but rather makes it lazy. And in that whirlpool of laziness everything that is great gets drawn in – and from there comes tiredness.'[20]It goes without saying that for Tagore, creativity was an act of gazing into life as 'an endless wonder'.[21]

The metaphysical sensibility underlying Tagore's pluralistic and empathetic philosophy was also a strategy of resisting the violence of the modern world through the moral empowerment of the living man. As Tagore acknowledged it, 'the living man has his true protection in his spiritual ideals, which have their vital connection with his life and grow with his growth.'[22] It is important to note that for Tagore the intellectual effort to disclose the whole of the human world in the dialogue of civilizations showed to a great measure that the spirit of harmony is the result of a combination of philosophical truths. Harmony, as Tagore understood it, was the highest expression of the human soul, a continuum of existential permeability and empathetic interconnectedness. This is how Tagore pictured the revival of Indianness, which had nothing to do with taking off the dust from a priceless heritage. According to him, what India needed was its own mind and its own spirit. He wrote: 'Once upon a time we were in possession of such a thing as our own mind in India. It was living. It thought, it felt, it expressed itself. It was receptive as well as productive.'[23] It is with this play of the Indian soul that Tagore tried to find a place for India in the creative unity of civilizations. Tagore would cry out:

> If we were to take for granted, what some people maintain, that Western culture is the only source of light for our mind, then it would be like depending for daybreak upon some star, which is the sun of a far distant sphere. The star may give us light, but not the day; it may give us direction in our voyage of exploration, but it can never open the full view of truth before our eyes. In fact, we can never use this cold starlight for stirring the sap in our branches and giving colour and bloom to our life.[24]

There is no shadow of doubt that Rabindranath Tagore was an Indian philosopher, but his commitment to human problems made him a philosopher in the service of humanity. For him, Indian awakening was to be constituted primarily by a philosophical awareness of the idea of India. He believed that as long as the Indian soul was limited by its mental ghettos, it would continue to be insignificant. While declaring his loyalty to Indian and western metaphysical thinking, Tagore condemned the unscrupulous forces of barbarity which kept 'ignited the fire of international jealousy, and [made] for universal incendiarism, for fearful orgy of devastation.'[25] In the face of this barbarism, with its human or divine face, which divided mankind, Tagore suggested the consciousness of unity. It was not only in his life as a poet, a philosopher or an educator that Tagore saw the work of this transcendent-spiritual consciousness. It is undeniable that for Tagore, in all human creative action, including politics, we must follow the voice of our conscience. Then, again, let us admit that what Tagore objected to in modern life was the absence of a moral compass which could provide us with the power of living in Truth. Following Tagore's paradigm of the end of violence, any struggle for a nonconformist and non-complacent world must enlarge and encompass the search for Truth.

What Tagore teaches us today is that the search for Truth is not a matter of faith but of moral power. It is culture and education that enable a community to understand what makes it meaningful under all circumstances. The vision of harmony between the east and the west was not a childish illusion that Tagore imposed upon himself and others. It was Tagore's invitation to mankind to come to its senses, an experience of the transcendental beyond the loss of metaphysical certainties. Tagore knew that in the long run, the power to awaken this new responsibility, towards something higher than everyday life, would be through directing humanity towards the moral and the spiritual order of the universe. Tagore's Socratic experience in life was a confirmation that philosophy as the practice of decency is possible. And there was even more: a Tagorean philosophy would be hard to imagine without the courage to breathe moral and spiritual impetus into everything. If the life of the spirit appealed to Tagore, it was because he wanted to help India and the world to mature and to be able to defy all the symptoms of the betrayal of humanity. He knew that as humanity progressed, it would discover that violence is not an absolute. For Tagore, to fight all forms of violence and to defeat it without the use of any new form of violence was a moral responsibility and a civilizational imperative. Ironically, the responsibility that Tagore was mentioning is now ours. Tagore knew well that the philosophical and political moment of non-violence he was talking about did not concern only his time, but, above all, it was a prayer for our forefathers and our grandchildren. The following message was written by Tagore in April 1920:

Let those who wish, try to burden the minds of the future with stones carrying the black memory of wrongs and their anger, but let us bequeath to the generations to come memorials of that only which we can revere – let us be grateful to our forefathers, who have left us the image of our Buddha, who conquered self, preached forgiveness and spread his love far and wide in time and space.[26]

It is only right to say that it was written for our time.

Notes

Foreword

1 Sabyasachi Bhattacharya, *Rabindranath Tagore: An Interpretation*, New Delhi: Penguin Books, 2011, pp. 43–4.

2 Ibid., pp. 43–4.

3 Publisher's note in Ruma Chakravarti, *Reliving Tagore: Poetry, Prose and Perceptions*, New Delhi: Vitasta Publishing House, 2016.

4 Michael Collins, *Empire, Nationalism and the Postcolonial World: Rabindranath Tagore's Writings on History, Politics and Society*, New Delhi: Routledge, 2014, p. 2.

5 Humayun Kabir in his introduction to Rabindranath Tagore, *Towards Universal Man*, New Delhi: Asia Publishing House, 1961, p. 21.

6 Bhattacharya, *Rabindranath Tagore*, p. 7.

7 Ibid.

8 Tagore, *Towards Universal Man*, p. 74.

9 Ibid.

10 Ibid., p. 39.

11 Rabindranath Tagore to C. F. Andrews, 4 August 1920, in *Letters to a Friend*, p. 262, cited in Tagore, *Towards Universal Man*.

12 Radha Chakravarty, ed., *Shades of Difference – Selected Writings of Rabindranath Tagore*, New Delhi: Social Science Press, 2015, p. 188.

13 Sarvepalli Radhakrishnan, *The Philosophy of Rabindranath Tagore*, New Delhi: Niyogi Books, 2015, p. xvii.

14 Ibid., p. 114.

15 Syeda Saiyidain Hameed, ed., *India's Maulana: Abul Kalam Azad*, New Delhi: Vikas Publishing House, 1990, p. 162.

16 *Speeches of Maulana Azad, 1947–1955*, New Delhi: Publications Division, Government of India, 1956, pp. 163–4.

17 Ibid., p. 163.

18 Uma Das Gupta, *Rabindranath Tagore – A Biography*, New Delhi: Oxford University Press, 2004, p. 1.

19 Ibid., p. 2.

20 Ibid.

21 Ibid., p. 3.
22 Amiya P. Sen, *Religion and Rabindranath Tagore*, New Delhi: Oxford University Press, 2014, p. xxii.
23 Ibid.
24 Ibid., p. xxiii.
25 'Dharma', first published in *Bharati*, March–April 1884. Later included in the collection *Alochana* (1885), reproduced in Rabindra Rachanabali (RR), vol. 15, pp. 28–34. Cited in Sen, *Religion and Rabindranath Tagore*, p. 9.
26 Rabindranath Tagore's letter to Indira Devi Chaudhurani, 11 February 1895, cited in Sen, *Religion and Rabindranath Tagore*, p. 188.
27 'Dharmer Saral Adarsha' (The Simple Ideals of Religion), first appeared in the journal *Bongodarshan*, January–February 1903, cited in Sen, *Religion and Rabindranath Tagore*, p. 41.
28 Rabindranath Tagore's letter to Hemantabala Devi, 14 June 1931, cited in Sen, *Religion and Rabindranath Tagore*, p. 208.
29 'Samanjasya' (Harmony), address delivered in Aghrayan, November–December 1908. Cited in Sen, *Religion and Rabindranath Tagore*, p. 104.
30 *Gora*, Rabindra Rachnabali (RR), vol. III, pp. 663–4, cited in Bhattacharya, *Rabindranath Tagore*, p. 126.
31 Ramin Jahanbegloo, 'Tagore and the Idea of Civilization', *IIC Quarterly*, vol. 34, no. 1, Summer, 2007, p. 65.
32 See the essay 'East and West' in *The English Writings of Rabindranath Tagore: Volume Two: Plays, Stories, Essays*, ed. Sisir Kumar Das, New Delhi: Sahitya Akademi, [1996] 2012, p. 536. Cited in Joyjit Ghosh, 'Translation as a Cultural Dialogue between the East and the West: Re-reading "The Nobel Prize Acceptance Speech" by Tagore', *Rupkatha Journal on Interdisciplinary Studies in Humanities*, vol. 11, no. 2, July–September, 2019, p. 1.
33 'East and West', p. 532.
34 http://www.nobelprize.org/nobel_prizes/literature/laureates/1913/press.html, cited in Ghosh, 'Translation as a Cultural Dialogue between the East and the West', p. 3.
35 Tagore, *Towards Universal Man*, p. 132.
36 Ibid.

37 Rabindranath Tagore in a foreword to a lecture by Maulvi Abdul Karim, *Islam's Contribution to Science and Civilization*, Calcutta: Goodword Books, 1935.

38 Ibid. p. 131.

39 'The Vicissitudes of Education', Tagore, *Towards Universal Man*, p. 40.

40 'The Problem of Education', in ibid., pp. 68–9.

41 Krishna Dutta and Andrew Robinson, ed., *Rabindranath Tagore – An Anthology*, London: Picador, 1997, p. 6.

42 Rabindranath Tagore, 'Gitanjali 35' from *Gitanjali (Song Offerings): A Collection of Prose Translations Made by the Author from the Original Bengali*, Introduction by W. B Yeats, London: MacMillan, 1913.

43 Tagore, *Towards Universal Man*, p. 202.

44 Ibid., p. 207.

45 'Problems in Education', cited in *Tagore on Education*, translated by Hiten Bhaya, Kolkatta: Dey's, 2012, p. 103.

46 Bhattacharya, *Rabindranath Tagore*, p. 111.

47 Ibid., p. 112.

48 *Speeches of Maulana Azad 1947–1955*, pp. 164–5.

49 Ibid., p. 165.

50 Rabindranath Tagore, *Towards Universal Man*, p. 249.

51 Bishwanth Ghosh, 'The Physics of Tagore: Promoting the Scientist in the Poet', *The Hindu*, 8 November 2019.

52 *Visva-Parichay*, Dedication to S. N. Bose, *Rabindra Rachnawali*, vol. XIII, pp. 519–22, cited in Bhattacharya, *Rabindranath Tagore*, p. 197.

53 Ibid.

54 Tagore, *Towards Universal Man*, p. 235.

55 Ibid., p. 233.

56 Ibid.

57 Ibid., p. 234.

58 I owe some of the issues raised here to the detailed introduction I wrote for my recent anthology *Indian Nationalism: The Essential Writings*, New Delhi: Aleph Book Company, 2017.

59 Aniruddha Ghoshal, 'Rabindranath Tagore in 1908: "I Will Never Allow Patriotism to Triumph over Humanity as Long as I Live', *Indian Express*, 2 December 2016.

60 Tagore, *Towards Universal Man*, p. 355.

61 Rabindranath Tagore, *Nationalism*, London: Macmillan, 1917, p. 123.
62 Ibid., pp. 133–4.
63 Ibid., pp. 103–4.
64 'Crisis in Civilization', in Tagore, *Towards Universal Man*, p. 357.
65 Tagore, *Nationalism*, p. 106.
66 Ibid., p. 114.
67 S Gopal, ed., *Jawaharlal Nehru An Anthology*, New Delhi: Oxford University Press, 1980, p. 590.
68 Dutta and Robinson, ed., *Rabindranath Tagore*, p. 2.
69 Ibid.
70 Ibid., pp. 2–3.
71 Sabyasachi Bhattacharya, ed., *The Mahatma and the Poet: Letters and Debates between Gandhi and Tagore 1915–1941*, New Delhi: National Book Trust, 1999, p. 31.
72 Bhattacharya, *Rabindranath Tagore*, p. 135.
73 Ibid.
74 Ibid., p. 136.
75 Humayun Kabir in his introduction to Tagore, *Towards Universal Man*, p. 34.
76 Bhattacharya, *Rabindranath* Tagore, p. 136.
77 *The Modern Review*, September 1925, cited in *The Collected Works of Mahatma Gandhi*, XXVIII (August–November 1925) New Delhi: Publications Division, p. 483.
78 Bhattacharya, *Rabindranath Tagore*, p. 136.
79 Ian Jack, 'Rabindranath Tagore Was a Global Phenomenon, So Why Is He Neglected?', *The Guardian*, 7 May 2011.
80 Ibid., p. 188.
81 Ibid., p. 35.
82 Tagore, *Towards Universal Man*, p. 343.

Introduction

1 Quayum A. Mohammad, ed., *Tagore, Nationalism and Cosmopolitanism: Perceptions, Contestations and Contemporary Relevance*, London: Routledge, 2020, p. 5.

2 Ibid., pp. 17–18.
3 Rabindranath Tagore, 'Letter to Hemantabala Devi, 19 October 1935', quoted in Amiya P. Sen, *Religion and Rabindranath Tagore: Select Discourses, Addresses, and Letters in Translation*, New Delhi: Oxford University Press, 2014, p. 224.
4 Sen, *Religion and Rabindranath Tagore*, Introduction, p. lxi.
5 Rabindranath Tagore, *Fireflies*, New Delhi: Atlantic, 2007. https://terebess.hu/english/tagore5.html.
6 Rabindranath Tagore, 'Harmony', in Sen, *Religion and Rabindranath Tagore*, p. 104.
7 Martha Nussbaum, 'Reinventing the Civil Religion: Comte, Mill, Tagore', in *Victorian Studies*, vol. 54, no. 1, Autumn 2011, pp. 24–5.
8 Martha Nussbaum, *The Clash Within: Democracy, Religious Violence, and India's Future*, Cambridge: Harvard University Press, 2007, p. 90.
9 Satish C. Aikant, 'Tagore, Cosmopolitanism and Secular Ethics', in Quayum A. Mohammad, ed., *Tagore, Nationalism and Cosmopolitanism*, p. 147.
10 Ibid., p. 154.
11 Ibid.
12 Rabindranath Tagore, 'World Consciousness', in Sen, *Religion and Rabindranath Tagore*, pp. 121–2.
13 Ibid., p. 122.
14 R. Nath, *India as Seen by Amir Khusrau (in 1318 A.D.)* Muhammad Fayyazuddin Ahmad Khan, ed., Jaipur: Historical Research Documentation Programme, 1981, p. 54.
15 Richard Stoneman, *The Greek Experience of India: From Alexander to the Indo-Greeks*, Princeton: Princeton University Press, 2019, p. 290.
16 Rabindranath Tagore, 'The Right Way to Realize God', in Sen, *Religion and Rabindranath Tagore*, p. 209.
17 Rabindranath Tagore, 'Harmony', in Sen, *Religion and Rabindranath Tagore*, p. 104.
18 Aikant, 'Tagore, Cosmopolitanism and Secular Ethics', in Quayum A. Mohammad, ed., *Tagore, Nationalism and Cosmopolitanism*, p. 149.
19 Richard Sorabji,'Tagore in Debate with Gandhi: Freedom as Creativity', in *Sophia*, no. 55, 2016, pp. 555–6.

20 Rabindranath Tagore, *Nationalism*, London: Penguin Book-Great Ideas, 2010, p. 20.
21 Rabindranath Tagore, 'The Religion of Man', in Sen, *Religion and Rabindranath Tagore*, pp. 166–7.
22 Rabindranath Tagore, 'Jeebondebata', in Sen, *Religion and Rabindranath Tagore*, p. 155.

Chapter 1

1 S. Chelliah, 'Mystic Vision and Cosmopolitan Outlook in Gitanjali', in *Language in India*, vol. 17, no. 3, March 2017, p. 52.
2 Sarvepalli Radhakrishnan, *East and West in Religion*, London: George Allen and Unwin, 1954, pp. 137–8.
3 Quoted in Sarvepalli Radhakrishnan, *The Philosophy of Rabindranath Tagore*, New Delhi: Nyogi Books, 2015, p. ix.
4 Rabindranath Tagore, *Sadhana*, Fairfield: First World Library-Literary Society, 2005, p. 42.
5 Rabindranath Tagore, *The Religion of Man*, quoted in Nagaraja P. Rao, 'The Religion of Tagore', in Mahendra Kulasrestha, *Tagore Centenary Volume*, Part I, Hoshiarpur: Vishveshvaranand V. R. Institute, 1961, p. 82.
6 Ibid., p. 86.
7 Ibid.
8 S. K. Paul, *The Complete Poems of Rabindranath Tagore's Gitanjali: Texts and Critical Evaluation*, New Delhi: Sarup, 2006, p. 80.
9 Rabindranath Tagore, *Of Myself*, trans. Devatta Joardar and Joe Winter, London: Anvil Press Poetry, 2006, p. 45.
10 Radhakrishnan, *The Philosophy of Rabindranath Tagore*, pp. 66–7.
11 Ibid., p. 66.
12 Kalyan Sen Gupta, *The Philosophy of Rabindranath Tagore*, New York: Routledge, 2016, p. 9.
13 Rabindranath Tagore, *The Gardener*, Madras: Macmillan Pocket edition, 1988, p. 112.
14 Kalyan, *The Philosophy of Rabindranath Tagore*, p. 10.

15 K. Krishnamoorthy, 'Tagore's Concept of Beauty', in Kulasrestha, *Tagore Centenary Volume*, p. 47.
16 Ibid., pp. 45–6.
17 Quoted by Richard Church, 'The Universal Man', in Sarvepalli Radhakrishnan, *A Centenary Volume Rabindranath Tagore(1861–1961)*, New Delhi: Sahitya Akademi, 1961, p. 131.
18 Rabindranath Tagore, *Personality*, London: Macmillan, 1917, p. 14.
19 Quoted in 'Tagore and Einstein', in Kulasrestha, *Tagore Centenary Volume*, p. 139.
20 Rabindranath Tagore, *Sadhana*, London: Macmillan, [1913] 1947, p. 8.
21 Rabindranath Tagore, *The Religion of Man*, London: George Allen & Unwin, [1931] 1970, p. 167.
22 Ezra Pound, 'A Review of Gitanjali', in Kulasrestha, *Tagore Centenary Volume*, p. 112.
23 Paul, *The Complete Poems of Rabindranath Tagore's Gitanjali*, pp.182–3.
24 Ibid., pp. 64–5.
25 Jose Chunkapura, *The God of Rabindranath Tagore: A Study of the Evolution of His Understanding of God*, Kolkata: Visva-Bharati, 2002, pp. 160–3.
26 Quoted in Ibid., p. 331.
27 Tagore, *Sadhana*, pp. 20–1.
28 Tagore, *Personality*, p. 80.
29 Quoted in Isaiah Berlin, *The Crooked Timber of Humanity*, ed. Henry Hardy, New York: Vintage Books, 1992, p. 37.
30 Rabindranath Tagore, *Selected Essays*, fifth edition, New Delhi: Rupa, 2010, p. 315.

Chapter 2

1 Rabindranath Tagore, 'Creative Unity' (1922), quoted in *Tagore: The Mystic Poets*, Woodstock: Sky Light Paths, 2004, pp. 31–2.
2 Quoted in Krishna Dutta, and Andrew Robinson, *Rabindranath Tagore: An Anthology*, New York: St. Martin's, 1997, p. 197.

3 Ibid., p. 213.
4 Dipannita Datta, 'Connecting Cultures: Rethinking Rabindranath Tagore's "Ideals of Education"', *Social Identities*, vol. 24, no. 3, 2018, p. 418.
5 Anthony X. Soares, ed., *Rabindranath Tagore: Lecture and Addresses*, London: Macmillan, 1970, pp. 104–5.
6 Amiya Chakravarty, *A Tagore Reader*, Boston: Beacon Press, 1961, p. 285.
7 Ibid., p. 36.
8 Rabindranath Tagore, *My Life in My Words*, ed. Uma Das Gupta, New Delhi: Penguin Books, 2006, p. 291.
9 Rabindranath Tagore, *Selected Essays*, fifth edition, New Delhi: Rupa, 2010, p. 440.
10 Datta, 'Connecting Cultures: Rethinking Rabindranath Tagore's "ideals of education', p. 420.
11 Quoted in Bidyut Chakrabarty, *Rabindranath Tagore's Ideational Challenges*, New Delhi: Bloomsbury Academic India, 2023, p. 6.
12 Rabindranath Tagore, *Selected Letters of Rabindranath Tagore*, Cambridge: Cambridge University Press, 1997, p. 515.
13 Quoted by Mulk Raj Anand, 'Tagore, Reconciler of East and West', in Sarvepalli Radhakrishnan, *A Centenary Volume Rabindranath Tagore (1861–1961)*, New Delhi: Sahitya Akademi, 1961, p. 68.
14 Chakrabarty, *Rabindranath Tagore's Ideational Challenges*, p. 14.
15 Rabindranath Tagore, 'The Religion of an Artist', quoted in Jose Chunkapura, *The God of Rabindranath Tagore: A Study of the Evolution of His Understanding of God*, Kolkata: Visva-Bharati, 2002, p. 268.
16 Quoted in Chunkapura, *The God of Rabindranath Tagore*, p. 291.
17 Ibid., p. 283.
18 Ibid., pp. 294–5.
19 Rabindranath Tagore, *Nationalism*, London: Penguin Book-Great Ideas, 2010, p. 43.
20 Quoted in Mulk Raj Ananad, 'Tagore, Reconciler of East and West', in Radhakrishnan, *A Centenary Volume Rabindranath Tagore (1861–1961)*, p. 73.
21 Rabindranath Tagore, *Address at Annual Convocation*, Calcutta: Calcutta University Press, 1937, p. 11.

22 Rabindranath Tagore, *Crisis in Civilization*, Calcutta: Visva-Bharati, [1941] 1964, pp. 12, 20.
23 Samik Bandyopadhyay, 'Tagore: Redefining Culture', in *India International Centre Quarterly*, vol. 38, no. 1, summer 2011, p. 39.
24 Ibid., pp. 35–6.
25 Rabindranath Tagore, 'The Religion of Man', in Sisir Kumar Das, ed., *English Writings of Rabindranath Tagore*, New Delhi: Sahitya Akademi, 2004, p. 111.
26 Quoted in Kalyan R. Salkar, *Rabindranath Tagore: His Impact on Indian Education*, New Delhi: Sterling, 1990, p. 23.
27 Rabindranath Tagore, 'A Poet's School', in *Towards Universal Man*, New Delhi: Asia Publishing House, 1961, pp. 300–1.

Chapter 3

1 Kathleen M. O'Connell, 'Freedom, Creativity, and Leisure in Education: Tagore in Canada, 1929', in *University of Toronto Quarterly*, vol. 77, no. 4, Fall 2008, p. 990.
2 Rabindranath Tagore, 'A Poet's School', in *Towards Universal Man*, New Delhi: Asia Publishing House, 1961, p. 300.
3 Ibid., p. 301.
4 Kathleen M. O'Connell, 'Visva-Bharati: Tagore's Response to Aggressive Nationalism?', in *Tagore, Nationalism and Cosmopolitanism: Perceptions, Contestations and Contemporary Relevance*, ed. Mohammad A. Quayum, New York: Routledge, 2020, p. 90.
5 Quoted in Kalyan R. Salkar, *Rabindranath Tagore: His Impact on Indian Education*, New Delhi: Sterling, 1990, p. 21.
6 Rabindranath Tagore, *My Life in My Words*, ed. Uma Das Gupta, New Delhi: Penguin Books, 2006, p. 196.
7 Rabindranath Tagore, 'The Story of History', in *Tagore on Education (Siksa)*, trans. Hiten Bhaya, Kolkata: Dey's, 2012, p. 98.
8 Rabindranath Tagore, 'System of Education', in *Tagore on Education (Siksa)*, pp. 182–3.

9 Ibid., p. 185.
10 Sabyasachi Bhattacharya, *Rabindranath Tagore: An Interpretation*, New Delhi: Penguin-Viking, 2011, pp. 191–2.
11 Rabindranath Tagore, 'Cooperative Education', in *Tagore on Education (Siksa)*, pp. 238–9.
12 Rabindranath Tagore, 'Co-operation', in *Towards Universal Man*, pp. 323, 339, 340.
13 Rabindranath Tagore, 'Unity of Education', in *Tagore on Education (Siksa)*, pp. 251–2.
14 Francis Assisi Samuel, 'Integrating Individual and Social Dimensions of Education: A Comparative Study of John Dewey and Rabindranath Tagore', PhD Thesis, Fordham University, New York, 1993, pp. 209–11.
15 Rabindranath Tagore, 'The Unity of Education', in *Towards Universal Man*, pp. 243, 245, 246.
16 Mohammad A. Quayum, 'Imagining "One World" Rabindranath Tagore's Critique of Nationalism', in ed. Mohammad A. Quayum, *Tagore, Nationalism and Cosmopolitanism: Perceptions, Contestations and Contemporary Relevance*, London: Routledge, 2020, p. 77.
17 Ibid., note 2, p. 82.
18 Rabindranath Tagore, 'Crisis in Civilization', in *Towards Universal Man*, p. 359.
19 Rabindranath Tagore, 'City and Village', in *Towards Universal Man*, pp. 306, 308.
20 Ibid., pp. 321–2.
21 Quoted in Bhattacharya, *Rabindranath Tagore: An Interpretation*, p. 195.
22 Ibid., p. 211.

Chapter 4

1 Ana Jelnikar, *Universalist Hopes in India and Europe: The Worlds of Rabindranath Tagore and Srecko Kosovel*, New Delhi: Oxford University Press, 2016, pp. 153–4.
2 Rabindranath Tagore, 'The Changing Age', in *Towards Universal Man*, New Delhi: Asia Publishing House, 1961, pp. 343–4.

3 Michael Collins, *Empire, Nationalism and the Postcolonial World: Rabindranath's Writings on History, Politics and Society*, New York: Routledge, 2012, p. 34.
4 Bhabatosha Datta, *Resurgent Bengal: Rammohun, Bankimchandra, Rabindranath*, Calcutta: Minerva Associates, 2000, p. 129.
5 Rabindranath Tagore, 'The Future of India', in *Modern Review*, vol. 9, no. 3, 1911, p. 240, quoted in Collins, *Empire, Nationalism and the Postcolonial World*, p. 65.
6 Letter from Rabindranath Tagore to C. F. Andrews (undated), quoted in Collins, *Empire, Nationalism and the Postcolonial World*, p. 67.
7 Rabindranath Tagore, 'My Interpretation of India's History: I', in *Modern Review*, vol. 14, no. 2, 1913, p. 113, quoted in Collins, *Empire, Nationalism and the Postcolonial World*, p. 65.
8 Rabindranath Tagore, 'The Master's Will Be Done', in *Towards Universal Man*, p. 194.
9 Rabindranath Tagore to C. F. Andrews, 7 September 1920, quoted in Krishna Dutta and Andrew Robinson, *Rabindranath Tagore: The Myriad-Minded Man*, New Delhi: Rupa, 2003, p. 237.
10 Ashis Nandy, *The Illegitimacy of Nationalism: Rabindranath Tagore and Politics of Self*, Delhi: Oxford University Press, 1994, p. 81.
11 S. Gopalakrishnan, 'Tagore on Nationalism: In Conversation with Prof. Ashis Nandy', *Sahapedia*, 2012.
12 Rabindranath Tagore, 'Jivansmriti', *Rabindra Rachnabali*, vol. 10, p. 67, quoted in Nandy, *The Illegitimacy of Nationalism*, p. 71.
13 Rabindranath Tagore, 'Personality', in *The English Writings of Rabindranath Tagore*, vol. 4, New Delhi: Atlantic, 2007, p. 377.
14 Martin Luther King, Jr., *Stride Toward Freedom*, New York: Harper & Row, 1958, p. 100.
15 Rabindranath Tagore, 'The Unity of Education', in *Towards Universal Man*, p. 246.
16 Rabindranath Tagore, 'The Nation', in *Modern Review*, vol. 22, no. 1, 1917, quoted in Collins, *Empire, Nationalism and the Postcolonial World*, p. 73.
17 Ibid., pp. 155–6.
18 Rabindranath Tagore, *Gora*, trans. Radha Chakravarty, New Delhi: Penguin Books, 2009, pp. 505–6.

19 Kalyan Kumar Chatterjee, 'Incognitos and Secret Sharers Patterns of Identity Tagore, Kipling and Forster', in *Indian Literature*, May–June, 1989, vol. 32, no. 3 (131), p. 118.
20 Jelnikar, *Universalist Hopes in India and Europe*, p. 93.
21 Rabindranath Tagore, *Nationalism*, London: Penguin Books, 2010, p. 38.
22 Ibid., pp. 43–4.
23 Rabindranath Tagore, 'The Religion of Man', in Sisir Kumar Das, ed., *The English Writings of Rabindranath Tagore*, vol. 3, New Delhi: Sahitya Akademi, 1931, p. 16.
24 Tagore to C. F. Andrews, 10 March 1918: C. F. Andrews, 'Letters to a Friend', in Kumar Das, ed., *The English Writings of Rabindranath Tagore*, p. 254.
25 Quoted in Collins, *Empire, Nationalism and the Postcolonial World*, p. 87.
26 Nandy, *The Illegitimacy of Nationalism*, pp. 80–1.
27 Rabindranath Tagore, 'Crisis in Civilization, in *Towards Universal Man*, pp. 358–9.

Chapter 5

1 Bindu Puri, 'Freedom and the Dynamics of the Self and the "Other"; Re-onstructing the Debate between Tagore and Gandhi', *Sophia*, vol. 52, no. 2, 2013, p. 337.
2 Ibid., p. 338.
3 K. Dutta and A. Robinson, *Rabindranath Tagore: The Myriad Minded Man*, London: Bloomsbury, 2008, p. 237.
4 Mahatma Gandhi, *All Men Are Brothers (Life and Thoughts of Mahatma Gandhi as Told in His Own Words)*, compiled and edited by Krishna Kripalani, Ahmedabad: Navajivan, 1971, p. 244.
5 Nirmal K. Bose, *Selections from Gandhi*, Ahmedabad: Navajivan, 1948, pp. 215–16.
6 Sabyasachi Bhattacharya, *The Mahatma and the Poet: Letters and Debates between Gandhi and Tagore, 1915–1941*, New Delhi: National Book Trust, 2005, p. 61.
7 Ibid., p. 85.
8 Rabindranath Tagore, *Greater India*, New Delhi: Rupa, 2003, p. 6.

9 Kalyan Sen Gupta, *The Philosophy of Rabindranath Tagore*, Hampshire: Ashgate, 2005, p. 38.
10 Tagore, *Greater India*, p. 18.
11 Rabindranath Tagore, 'Society and State', in *Towards Universal Man*, New Delhi: Asia Publishing House, 1961, pp. 65–6.
12 Bhattacharya, *The Mahatma and the Poet*, pp. 2–3.
13 Ibid., p. 49.
14 Ibid., pp. 21–2.
15 Rabindranath Tagore, 'The Call of Truth', in *Towards Universal Man*, pp. 268, 270.
16 Ibid., p. 255.
17 Bindu, 'Freedom and the Dynamics of the Self and the "Other"', p. 341.
18 Romain Rolland to Rabindranath Tagore, 2 March 1923, quoted in Bhattacharya, *The Mahatma and the Poet*, p. 37.
19 Bhattacharya, *The Mahatma and the Poet*, p. 23.
20 Ibid., p. 46.
21 Ibid., pp. 57–8.
22 Tagore, 'The Striving for Swaraj', in *Towards Universal Man*, p. 282.
23 Tagore, 'The Call of Truth', in *Towards Universal Man*, p. 269.
24 Bhattacharya, *The Mahatma and the Poet*, p. 90.
25 Tagore, 'The Call of Truth', in *Towards Universal Man*, p. 272.

Conclusion

1 Priyam Marik, 'Why Are Bengalis Endlessly Obsessed with Rabindranath Tagore?', *Telegraph Online*, 9 May 2023.
2 Rabindranath Tagore, 'What Then?', in *Towards Universal Man*, New Delhi: Asia Publishing House, 1961, p. 86.
3 Ibid., p. 99.
4 Rabindranath Tagore, 'The Centre of Indian Culture', in *Towards Universal Man*, p. 226.
5 Quoted it in Romain Rolland, *Mahatma Gandhi: The Man Who Became One with the Universal Being*, trans. Catherine D. Groth, New Delhi: Publications Division, 1969, p. 82.
6 See George Steiner, *The Poetry of Thought: From Hellenism to Celan*, New York: New Directions Book, 2011, p. 202.

7 Rabindranath Tagore, 'Co-operation', in *Towards Universal Man*, pp. 324–5.
8 Alain, 'Commentaire sur "La Jeune Parque" ' in George, *The Poetry of Thought*, p. 8.
9 Rabindranath Tagore, *The English Writings of Rabindranath Tagore*, ed. Sisir Kumar Das, vol. 1, New Delhi: Sahitya Akademi, 2004, p. 46.
10 Tagore, 'What Then?', in *Towards Universal Man*, pp. 88–9.
11 Hannah Arendt, *The Freedom to Be Free*, New York: Penguin Books, 2018, p. 35.
12 Rabindranath Tagore, *Nationalism*, New York: Penguin Books, 2010, pp. 9–10.
13 Ibid., p. 69.
14 Rabindranath Tagore, 'A Hymn to India', in *Indian Literature*, vol. 1, no. 2, April–September, 1958, p. 1.
15 Rabindranath Tagore, 'Reflections on Non-cooperation and Cooperation', *Modern Review*, May, 1921, quoted in Sabyasachi Bhattacharya, *The Mahatma and the Poet: Letters and Debates between Gandhi and Tagore, 1915–1941*, New Delhi: National Book Trust, 2005, p. 60.
16 Rabindranath Tagore, *The Diary of a Westward Voyage*, Calcutta: Asia Publishing House, 1962, pp. 76–7.
17 Ibid., p. 74.
18 Tagore, *Nationalism*, p. 11.
19 Chinmoy Guha, *Bridging East and West: Rabindranath Tagore and Romain Rolland Correspondence (1919–1940)*, New Delhi: Oxford University Press, 2018, p. 23.
20 Rabindranath Tagore, 'Letter to Rani Mahalanobis, July 1929', quoted in Sudhir Kakar, *Young Tagore: The Making of a Genius*, New Delhi: Penguin-Viking, 2013, p. 54.
21 Ibid., p. 183.
22 Tagore, *Nationalism*, p. 21.
23 Rabindranath Tagore, 'Creative Unity', in *The English Writings of Rabindranath Tagore*, vol. 4, New Delhi: Atlantic, 2007, p. 643.
24 Ibid., p. 651.
25 Guha, *Bridging East and West*, p. 48.
26 Rabindranath Tagore, *The English Writings of Rabindranath Tagore*, vol. 8, New Delhi: Atlantic, 2007, p. 1025.

Bibliography

Andrews, C. F., ed., *Letters to a Friend: Rabindranath Tagore's Letters to C. F. Andrews*, New Delhi: Rupa, 2002.

Arendt, Hannah, *The Freedom to Be Free*, New York: Penguin Books, 2018.

Aronson, Alex, *Rabindranath Tagore through Western Eyes*, Calcutta: Rddhi, [1943] 1978.

Ayyub, Abu Sayeed, *Modernism and Tagore*, trans. Amitava Ray, New Delhi: Sahitya Akademi, 1995.

Berlin, Isaiah, *The Crooked Timber of Humanity*, ed. Henry Hardy, New York: Vintage Books, 1992.

Bhattacharya, Debraj, ed., *Of Matters Modern: The Experience of Modernity in Colonial and Post-Colonial South Asia*, Calcutta: Seagull Books, 2008.

Bhattacharya, Sabyasachi, *Rabindranath Tagore: An Interpretation*, New Delhi: Penguin Viking, 2011.

Bhattacharya, Sabyasachi, *The Mahatma and the Poet: Letters and Debates between Gandhi and Tagore, 1915–1941*, New Delhi: National Book Trust, 2005.

Bose, Nemai Sadhan, ed., *Rabindranath Tagore in Perspective: A Bunch of Essays*, Calcutta: Visva-Bharati, 1989.

Bose, Nirmal K., *Selections from Gandhi*, Ahmedabad: Navajivan, 1948.

Chakrabarty, Bidyut, *Rabindranath Tagore's Ideational Challenges*, New Delhi: Bloomsbury, 2023.

Chakravarty, Amiya, *A Tagore Reader*, Boston: Beacon, 1961.

Chunkapura, Jose, *The God of Rabindranath Tagore: A Study of the Evolution of His Understanding of God*, Kolkata: Visva-Bharati, 2002.

Collins, Michael, *Empire, Nationalism and the Postcolonial World: Rabindranath's Writings on History, Politics and Society*, New York: Routledge, 2012.

Colm, Hogan Patrick, and Pandit Lalita, eds, *Rabindranath Tagore: Universality and Tradition*, Madison, NJ: Fairleigh Dickinson University Press, 2003.

Datta, Bhabatosha, *Resurgent Bengal: Rammohun, Bankimchandra, Rabindranath*, Calcutta: Minerva Associates, 2000.

Dutta, Krishna, and Andrew Robinson, *Rabindranath Tagore: An Anthology*, New York: St. Martin's, 1997.

Dutta, Krishna, and Andrew Robinson, *Rabindranath Tagore: The Myriad-Minded Man*, New Delhi: Rupa, 2003.

Dutta, Krishna, and Andrew Robinson, eds, *Selected Letters of Rabindranath Tagore*, Cambridge: Cambridge University Press, 2005.

Gandhi, Mahatma, *All Men Are Brothers (Life and Thoughts of Mahatma Gandhi as Told in His Own Words*), compiled and edited by Krishna Kripalani, Ahmedabad: Navajivan, 1971.

Guha, Chinmoy, *Bridging East & West: Rabindranath Tagore and Romain Rolland Correspondence (1919–1940)*, New Delhi: Oxford University Press, 2018.

Gupta, Kalyan Sen, *The Philosophy of Rabindranath Tagore*, Hampshire: Ashgate, 2005.

Gupta, Uma Das, ed., *A Difficult Friendship: Letters of Edward Thompson and Rabindranath Tagore 1913–1940*, New Delhi: Oxford University Press, 2003.

Gupta, Uma Das, ed., *Rabindranath Tagore: My Life in My Words*, New Delhi: Penguin Viking, 2006.

Jelnikar, Ana, *Universalist Hopes in India and Europe: The Worlds of Rabindranath Tagore and Srecko Kosovel*, New Delhi: Oxford University Press, 2016.

King, Martin Luther, Jr, *Stride Toward Freedom*, New York: Harper & Row,1958.

Kulasrestha, Mahendra, ed., *Tagore Centenary Volume*, Part I, Hoshiarpur: Vishveshvaranand V.R. Institute, 1961.

Nandy, Ashis, *The Illegitimacy of Nationalism: Rabindranath Tagore and Politics of Self*, New Delhi: Oxford University Press, 1994.

Paul, S. K., *The Complete Poems of Rabindranath Tagore: Gitanjali: Texts and Critical Evaluation*, New Delhi: Sarup & Sons, 2006.

Quayum, Mohammad A., ed., *Tagore, Nationalism and Cosmopolitanism: Perceptions, Contestations and Contemporary Relevance*, London: Routledge, 2020.

Radakrishnan, Sarvepalli, *A Centenary Volume Rabindranath Tagore (1861–1961*), New Delhi: Sahitya Akademi, 1961.

Sahu, Monideepa, *Rabindranath Tagore: The Renaissance Man*, New Delhi: Puffin Books, 2013.

Salkar, Kalyan R., *Rabindranath Tagore: His Impact on Indian Education*, New Delhi: Sterling, 1990.

Samuel, Francis Assisi, 'Integrating Individual and Social Dimensions of Education: A Comparative Study of John Dewey and Rabindranath Tagore', Ph.D. Thesis, New York: Fordham University, 1993.

Sen, Amiya P., *Religion and Rabindranath Tagore: Select Discourses, Addresses, and Letters in Translation*, New Delhi: Oxford University Press, 2014.

Soares, Anthony X., ed., *Rabindranath Tagore: Lecture and Addresses*, London: Macmillan, 1970.

Steiner, George, *The Poetry of Thought: From Hellenism to Celan*, New York: New Directions Books, 2011.

Stoneman, Richard, *The Greek Experience of India: From Alexander to the Indo-Greeks*, Princeton: Princeton University Press, 2019.

Tagore, Rabindranath, *The English Writings of Rabindranath Tagore*, ed. Sisir Kumar Das, New Delhi: Sahitya Akademi, 2004.

Tagore, Rabindranath, *The English Writings of Rabindranath Tagore*, New Delhi: Atlantic, 2007.

Tagore, Rabindranath, *Gora*, trans. Radha Chakravarty, New Delhi: Penguin Books, 2009.

Tagore, Rabindranath, *Nationalism*, New York: Penguin Books, 2010.

Tagore, Rabindranath, *The Diary of a Westward Voyage*, Calcutta: Asia Publishing House, 1962.

Tagore, Rabindranath, 'A Hymn to India', in *Indian Literature*, vol. 1, no. 2, April–September, 1958, pp. 1–3.

Tagore, Rabindranath, *Towards Universal Man*, New Delhi: Asia Publishing House, 1961.

Tagore, Rabindranath, *Personality*, London: Macmillan, 1917.

Tagore, Rabindranath, *Fireflies*, New York: Macmillian, 1928. https://archive.org/details/fireflies0000tago.

Tagore, Rabindranath, *Greater India*, New Delhi: Rupa, 2003.

Tagore, Rabindranath, *Sadhana*, London: Macmillan, 1926.

Tagore, Rabindranath, *Crisis in Civilization*, Calcutta: Visva-Bharati, [1941] 1964.

Tagore, Rabindranath, 'System of Education', in *Tagore on Education (Siksa)*, trans. Hiten Bhaya, Kolkata: Dey's, 2012, p. 98.

Tagore, Rabindranath, *Address at Annual Convocation*, University of Calcutta, 13 February 1937, Calcutta: Calcutta University Press, 1937.

Tagore, Rabindranath, *Selected Letters of Rabindranath Tagore*, Cambridge: Cambridge University Press, 1997.

Tagore, Rabindranath, *Rabindranath Tagore: An Anthology*, London: Picador, 1997.

Tagore, Rabindranath, *Sadhana*, trans. Satish Chandra Ray, Ajit Kumar Chakravarty and Surendranath Tagore, New Delhi: Rupa, [1913] 2002.

Tagore, Rabindranath, *Creative Unity*, New Delhi: Rupa, [1922] 2002.

Tagore, Rabindranath, *Talks in China: Lectures Delivered in April and May 1924*, New Delhi: Rupa, [1925] 2002.

Tagore, Rabindranath, *The Religion of Man*, New Delhi: Rupa, [1931] 2002.

Tagore, Rabindranath, *Journey to Persia and Iraq: 1932*, Santiniketan: Visva-Bharati, 2003.

Tagore, Rabindranath, *Selected Essays*, fifth edition, New Delhi: Rupa, 2010.

Tagore, Rabindranath, *My Life in My Words*, ed. Uma Das Gupta, New Delhi: Penguin Books, 2006.

Tagore, Rabindranath, *Tagore: The Mystic Poets*, Woodstock: Sky Light Paths, 2004.

Tagore, Rabindranath, *The Religion of Man*, London: George Allen & Unwin, [1931] 1970.

Tagore, Rabindranath, *Gitanjali: Song Offerings*, trans. by the author, New Delhi: UBSP, 2003.

Tagore, Rabindranath, *Selected Poems*, ed. Sukanta Chaudhuri, New Delhi: Oxford University Press, 2004.

Tagore, Rabindranath, *The Home and the World*, trans. Surendranath Tagore, London: Penguin Books, 2005.

Tagore, Rabindranath, *On Art and Aesthetics*, Kolkata: Subarnarekha, 2005.

Tagore, Rabindranath, *Of Myself (Atmaparichay)*, trans. Devadatta Joardar and Joe Winter, Kolkata: Visva-Bharati, 2006.

Tagore, Rabindranath, *Selected Short Stories*, ed. Sukanta Chaudhuri, New Delhi: Oxford University Press, 2006.

Tagore, Rabindranath, *Sesher Kobita; The Last Poem*, trans. Anindita Mukhopadhyay, New Delhi: Rupa, 2007.

Tagore, Rabindranath, *Classic Rabindranath Tagore*, New Delhi: Penguin Books, 2011.

Thompson, Edward John, *Rabindranath Tagore: Poet and Dramatist*, Delhi: Oxford University Press, 1991.

Index